# A HISTORY OF
# SAILING
# IN 100 OBJECTS

BARRY PICKTHALL

# A HISTORY OF
# SAILING
# IN 100 OBJECTS

BLOOMSBURY

LONDON · OXFORD · NEW YORK · NEW DELHI · SYDNEY

**Adlard Coles Nautical**
An imprint of Bloomsbury Publishing Plc

| | |
|---|---|
| 50 Bedford Square | 1385 Broadway |
| London | New York |
| WC1B 3DP | NY 10018 |
| UK | USA |

*www.bloomsbury.com*
*www.adlardcoles.com*

ADLARD COLES, ADLARD COLES NAUTICAL and the Buoy logo are trademarks
of
Bloomsbury Publishing Plc
First published 2016
© Barry Pickthall 2016

British Library Cataloguing-in-Publication Data
A catalogue record for this book is available from the British Library.
Library of Congress Cataloguing-in-Publication data has been applied for.

ISBN: HB: 978-1-4729-1885-7
ePDF: 978-1-4729-1887-1
ePub: 978-1-4729-1886-4

4  6  8  10  9  7  5  3

Designed by Nicola Liddiard, Nimbus Design
Printed and bound in China by RR Donnelley Asia Printing Solutions Limited

Bloomsbury Publishing Plc makes every effort to ensure that the papers
used in the manufacture of our books are natural, recyclable products made
from wood grown in well-managed forests. Our manufacturing processes conform
to the environmental regulations of the country of origin.

To find out more about our authors and books visit www.bloomsbury.com.
Here you will find extracts, author interviews, details of forthcoming
events and the option to sign up for our newsletters.

# Introduction

The oldest boat ever discovered is the Pesse canoe, a dugout made from pine thought to date back to 8200 BC, and undoubtedly powered by paddles. It seems to have taken another 3000 years for the Mesopotamians and Ancient Egyptians to come up with the concept of using the wind to propel their craft. Sailing boats became the means to transport goods and people across oceans and between trading empires. They also enabled warring powers to undertake campaigns at sea as well as on land. And as boatbuilders and mariners became more skilled, sailing boats became ever more sophisticated and complex.

Although arranged chronologically, this book is not a history of the sailing boat. Rather it looks at a number of items and events that have marked a turning point in technological development or human achievement at sea. There are plenty of ships and smaller craft, from the superb lines of the Viking warship at Oseberg to the equally magnificent – but disastrous – Swedish ship, *Vasa* and the clipper ships *Ann McKim* and *Cutty Sark*, that bookmark their era to dinghies from the tiny Optimist to the first planing dinghies such as the International 14 *Avenger*.

Other objects included are far smaller but equally crucial in the development of sailing, from the cross staff, astrolabe and sextant that allowed increasingly sophisticated navigation, to the radar and GPS that followed and now allow sailors to pinpoint their position with great precision. Significant turning points in more workmanlike items such as blocks, sails and spars are also covered.

This broad approach allows for an eclectic range of 'objects' to be included. So while a lemon may seem an eccentric inclusion, the essential role of citrus fruit in combating the scourge of scurvy on long voyages is undisputed. Other objects such as scrimshaw, grog and the sou'wester all shine a light on the changing lives of sailors.

Essentially though, this book is a celebration of sailing, the boats in which we sail and the people who sail them. We hope you enjoy it.

# Contents

Model made by French prisoners from the
Napoleonic wars whilst captive in Britain,

# 1 : Naqada II pot

## 3,500 BC

Who invented the sail? We'll probably never know for sure, but there's a simple dynamic that puts Egypt at the top of the list of candidates for this honour. And it all comes down to gravity. It was the life-giving force of the River Nile that created one of the world's most advanced civilisations in Ancient Egypt. Archaeological evidence suggests that the Egyptians may have used boats to navigate that river in at least 4000 BC, and probably much earlier. But like all rivers, the Nile flows only one way: pulled by gravity to the sea. So while the Egyptians would have had a swift ride north, to the Mediterranean, it would have been heavier going heading south, inland, against the current.

Happily, the gods that created this beautiful oasis also devised a solution to this problem and arranged for the prevailing wind to come from the north. The early navigators just had to ride this current going north, and stick up a palm leaf to let the wind blow them back south. Palm leaves were eventually replaced with cloth, and thus the first sail was (probably) born.

Many depictions of boats have been found in the area, including the 2004 discovery of a half-boat painted on a granite pebble in around 7000 BC, thought to be the oldest image of a boat in the world. But the first clear depiction of a *sail* is on the Naqada II pot, painted in Egypt in the late Predynastic period around 3600–3250 BC. It's a wonderfully loose, carefree image of a boat sailing across water, presumably a river, with the check pattern at the top portraying a riverbank. The boat carries a square sail, so it would only ever be any use for going downwind, but nevertheless ideal for sailing back up the Nile after a visit up north, or for carrying produce to a market further upriver.

Historians are undecided about when the Ancient Egyptians switched from reed to wooden boats, or indeed whether they were building both types all along. Judging by the position of this boat's sail, the boat is likely to have been of wooden construction, since a reed hull wouldn't have taken the strains of a sail placed so close to an end. Also, this boat's hull shape is asymmetrical; reed boats are, by definition, symmetrical and shown as such in most contemporary images, so we therefore have to assume that the depiction on the Naqada II pot is of a wooden boat.

Whole fleets of boats have been discovered carved in rocks at Nag el-Hamdulab in southern Egypt (3200–3100 BC), and a square sail is clearly portrayed on an incense burner found in Nubia (3200–3000 BC). But the boat shown on the Naqada II pot is in a class of its own. Depicted for its own sake, rather than as a detail in a bigger picture, it gives us our first sense of the pleasure and excitement of sailing that would capture future generations of sailors and turn it into a worldwide sport.

On the Naquada II pot, the boats have palm branches
at the prow and what appear to be oars at the
bottom with two cabins on the deck. Each cabin has
a female figure flanked by smaller male figures –
possibly representing a goddess and her priests.

1 : NAQADAR II POT, 3,500 BC

# 2 : The ships of Wadi Gawasis

## 1,800 BC

The Egyptian female pharaoh Hatshepsut reigned (or, strictly speaking, co-reigned) for 15 years between c.1473–1458 BC, during which she re-established several trade routes and with the resulting wealth, ordered the construction of more buildings and statues than any of her predecessors.

One of her most celebrated achievements was an expedition to the Land of Punt in about 1490 BC, where she bought gold, ivory, incense and myrrh trees and returned them to Egypt, supposedly the first time trees had been transported from one country to another. The 2,000-mile (3,218km) round trip is described in detail in carved reliefs on the walls of Hatshepsut's mortuary temple at Deir el-Bahari, on the west bank of the Nile, and includes images of the five ships she took with her.

Hatshepsut's expedition to the Land of Punt is probably the first nautical voyage depicted in art, and it soon acquired a semi-mythical status – all the more, since no one could agree on the actual location of Punt, although it is assumed to have been on the Horn of Africa, in modern-day Eritrea or Yemen.

Then, in 2005 the remains of a shipyard of that era were discovered near the Red Sea. Ship's timbers, coils of rope, anchors and cargo boxes were unearthed at six man-made caves at Wadi Gawasis, near Port Safaga on the Red Sea. Hieroglyphs on several boxes indicated that they came from the Land of Punt, suggesting the site was also used as a depot for trading ships heading south. The timbers contained shipworms only found at sea, advancing the theory that the vessels had been on a journey of approximately six months – about the time it would take to sail to the Horn of Africa and back.

No one is implying these are the remains of the actual ships that took part on that fabled expedition, but they are certainly their direct contemporaries, making them the oldest remains of sea-going ships anywhere in the world. Older boats have been discovered, but they are all of smaller craft, such as canoes and rafts. Suddenly, a story from 3500 years ago deduced from descriptions and circumstantial evidence was given physical substance. It was almost as if the mythological land of Atlantis had finally been discovered.

A French television company saw the potential, commissioning a team of archaeologists and a naval architect to recreate the original voyage in ships built to the same designs of the day, an amalgam of the craft depicted in Hatshepsut's mortuary and the remains found at Wadi Gawasis. The 66ft (30m)-long by 16ft (4.9m)-wide vessel, *Min of the Desert*, was launched in October 2008 and set sail across the Red Sea. Unlike its historic predecessor, its journey was cut short after just 150 miles (241km) due to political tensions and the danger of piracy. As such, *Min of the Desert* never left Egyptian waters. Hatshepsut would not have been impressed.

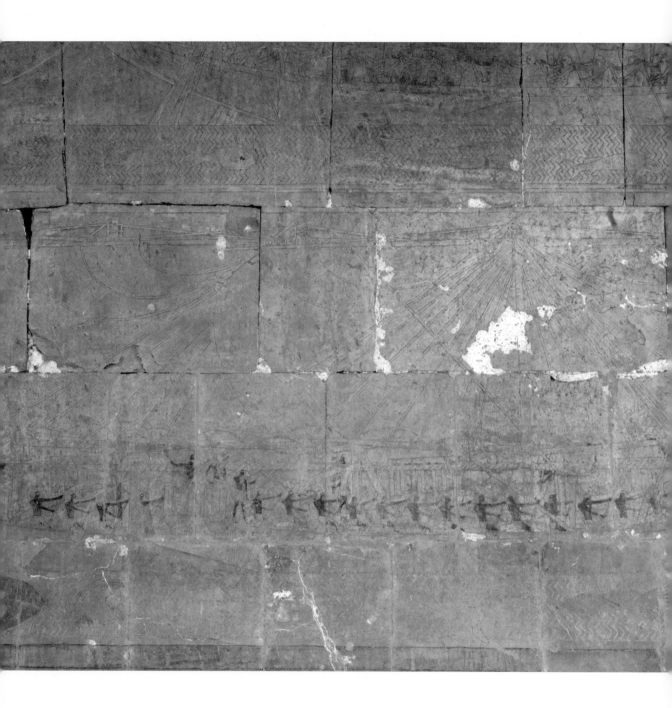

Wall art depicting Egyptian ships and soldiers on the
expedition to the Land of Punt. They are found in the
Temple of Hatshepsut, dating from c. 1490 BC, 18th
Dynasty, New Kingdom, Deir el-Bahari, Egypt.

**2 : WADI GAWASIS SHIPS, 1,800 BC**

# 3 : The Pharos at Alexandria

## 280 BC

The use of lights as aids to navigation goes back as far as the eighth century BC, with references to beacons lit on hilltops to guide ships appearing in Homer's *Iliad* and *Odyssey*. But the first-known lighthouse, the Pharos of Alexandria, in Egypt, was completed in 280 BC. Its architect, Sostratus of Cnidus, began the project during the reign of the Macedonian ruler Ptolemy I Soter and it was finished under the watchful eye of Soter's son, Ptolemy II.

Standing at 350ft (107m) high, the lighthouse was second only to the pyramids of Giza as the tallest manmade structure of ancient times. Taking its name from the island on which it was built, the lighthouse was regarded by the ancient Greeks as one of the Seven Wonders of the World. It was certainly a technological triumph.

The lighthouse was constructed in three stages: a square base that supported a 100ft (30.5m) square tier, topped by a 15ft (5m) octagonal storey. This in turn supported an 85ft (26m) cylindrical tier with the fire at the top. It was a masterpiece of engineering, with metal used to reinforce the huge blocks of stone. To keep the brazier burning, workers carried wood up a spiral ramp within the building.

The Pharos lighthouse outlasted many of the other ancient wonders, eventually succumbing to an earthquake sometime during the 14th century.

In 1994, French archaeologist Jean-Yves Empereur was commissioned to chart the area prior to the construction of a concrete breakwater. He discovered hundreds of huge masonry blocks and statues, including a sculpture thought to depict Ptolemy II dating back to the third century BC. Work on the concrete breakwater was abandoned and the area was instead turned into an underwater park, where scuba divers can now explore the lighthouse's relics and remains.

The Pharos lighthouse was believed to have been built
in three stages. The lowest part was square, the next
octagonal, and the top cylindrical. The top was reached
via a wide spiral ramp where a fire was lit at night.

# 4 : Oseberg Viking longship

## 846 AD

For 300 years the Vikings terrorised Northern Europe. They attacked coastal towns across Germany, France, England and Ireland, and made forays into the Mediterranean and the Black Sea. And it wasn't just the occasional rogue Viking heading off to fill his coffers – some 600 Viking ships attacked Hamburg in AD 845, and later that year another 130 poured up the Seine River in France. Viking groups settled as far afield as Iceland and probably landed in America some 500 years before Columbus got there.

The reason for their success? Their boats, or longships, were formidable instruments, far superior to any other vessels in existence at the time. Usually made from solid oak with long, overlapping planks sweeping up dramatically at either end, longships were a world away from the lumbering vessels the rest of Europe was still plodding around in. Longships were lightweight fantasies, the construction of which should not have been possible with the tools and materials available at the time, making them a testament to the great skill and imagination of Scandinavian boatbuilders.

On the water, longships were like overgrown dinghies, skimming over waves rather than crashing through them like most other European vessels. They were seaworthy enough to cross the open oceans at 12 knots and yet shallow enough to land on any beach and sneak up any river, rowed silently into enemy territory under cover of night. Nowhere was beyond their reach (some Vikings even carried their ships across land to reach their next target), and they almost always arrived without warning. And, once they had seized whatever they wanted, the invaders could load their ships with loot and set off, safe in the knowledge that no one could catch up with them.

Several surviving Viking longships have been discovered, but the jewel in the crown is the *Oseberg*. Found by a Norwegian farmer on his land to the west of the Oslofjord, this 70ft 'karv' was wider and lower than the longships engaged in warfare, suggesting it was used either for carrying cargo or ceremonial purposes. The forward stem is decorated from the keel upwards with intricate relief carvings of animals and topped by a snake's head, a full 16ft (4.9m) high.

Whatever the ship's original purpose, it ended its active service as a coffin in a classic Viking burial; the remains of two women were found inside the boat, one around 70–80 years old, the other around 50. Their corpses were surrounded by personal effects, including tapestries, clothes, shoes and combs, as well as practical objects, such as kitchen utensils and farming equipment. There were also four sledges, five beds, two tents, 15 horses, six dogs and two small cows. Everything they needed for the next life.

The Oseberg ship is housed near Oslo in a cross-shaped building with two other longships. Visiting them can feel like an almost spiritual experience.

# 5 : Bosun's pipe

## 1248

The bosun's pipe, or boatswain's whistle, was the method first used by England's Royal Navy to signal specific orders to a ship's crew above the sounds of the sea and gunfire. Blown by the boatswain, the pipe consists of a narrow tube (the gun) that directs air over a metal sphere – the buoy, which has a hole in the top – over which the player opens and closes his/her hand to change the sound's pitch. The remainder of the pipe consists of a flat piece of metal (the keel) beneath the gun and the key ring (the shackle), which connects a long silver or brass chain that sits around the player's collar when in ceremonial uniform. The pipe whistle is now used as a traditional bugle call to 'pipe' aboard flag-rank officers and important guests, as well as mark Evening Colours. It is the official badge of the quartermaster, chief boatswain's mate and boatswain's mate in many navies around the world.

---

### COMMANDS

**HAUL** Warship crews were not allowed to sing, so the pipe was used to coordinate the sailors. The low note signals a pause and is preparatory, and the high note for pulling on the line.

**THE SIDE OR AWAY GALLEY** This goes back to the tradition of hoisting officers aboard ship in a chair. It is a combination of haul and a command to lower, and remains in use as an honour bestowed upon officers when embarking or disembarking.

**AWAY BOATS** Orders a ship's boats to leave the ship's side. Call the boatswain's mates: Boatswain's gang to report.

**ALL HANDS ON DECK** The entire crew to assemble on deck. Word to be passed: Command for silence, an order to follow.

**PIPE DOWN** Dismissal of all the crew not on watch.

**SWEEPERS** End of the working day. Ostensibly sailors would 'sweep up' in preparation for departure the following day.

**PIPE TO ANY MEAL** Pipe all hands, followed by long heave around (mess gear), and long pipe down.

**STILL** Used to call the crew to attention when two warships passed each other, and the crew of the junior ship salutes the senior ship.

**CARRY ON** Used after the still, to dismiss the crew back to their duties.

**GENERAL CALL** Piped before an announcement.

**OFFICER OF THE DAY** Calls the Officer of the Day to the gangway.

The bosun's pipe is also sometimes referred to as the
'bosun's call'. The form of the whistle has remained very
similar since it was first invented in the 13th century.

# 6 : Carta Pisana

## 1270

It looks somewhat reminiscent of a geometric doodle drawn on an old tea towel and, at first sight, this 740-year-old piece of hide is pretty incomprehensible. Look more closely though, and you will see the first 'inside out' view of Europe, for the Carta Pisana is the first-known maritime chart, drawn from the point of view of the sea rather than the land. In fact, it's of no use to the land traveller, since only coastal points are marked and the landmasses themselves are notably inaccurate.

For the sea traveller, however, the chart is instantly usable. Give a copy to a sailor and using a pair of parallel rules, he/she will be able to read off a course between any of the almost 1,000 ports named without the slightest trouble. For this maritime masterpiece is a portolan chart, from the Italian portolano, or 'relating to ports', the forebear of all later nautical charts.

Its only purpose is to chart the relative position of the ports and the distances between them – there's no attempt to depict the areas' topography, and even the shapes of the landmasses are relatively unimportant. The star-shaped grids represent the 16 points of a basic compass (north, north-east by north, north-east, etc.) and allow the course to be read off anywhere on the chart – just like a compass rose on later successors. The smaller circles at top and right are scales, which allow the navigator to read off distances.

The Carta Pisana is both simple and remarkably accurate. Digital analysis of the chart, which was used to transpose it over a modern map of the region portrayed, showed an overall error in scale of just 1.4 per cent (excluding the Atlantic Coast and the Black Sea). The area portrayed with the greatest error is the Adriatic, which was drawn 7.3 per cent larger than it actually is. Exclude that too, and the chart has only a 1.1 per cent error in scale. Less impressive is the orientation of the chart, which needs to be rotated 9.6 degrees anti-clockwise to be accurate.

The exact origins of the Carta Pisana are not known, although as its name suggests, the chart was found in Pisa and is almost certainly Italian, coming either from Genoa, Venice or Pisa itself. Given the concentration of names in the Tyrrhenian Sea, it seems likely that it was in fact drafted in Genoa. The exact age is unknown, though it's generally accepted that it must be between 1258, when the port of Manfredonia was founded, and 1291, when the port of Acre fell to Muslim forces (a cross is drawn by its name). The final piece of evidence comes with the first mention of such a detailed chart, on a Genoese ship in 1270.

During the 17th century, sea charts based on the Mercator projection replaced the portolan. The Dutch dominated chartmaking in the early years, followed by France and Great Britain, which set up hydrographic offices in 1720 and 1795 respectively.

The Carta Pisana is one of around 180 nautical charts that have
survived from the period 1200–1400 and virtually nothing before
that is recorded. It seems that ancient navigators such as the
Phoenicians may well have made charts or sketches in the course of
navigation but since they were considered 'instruments' for the trip
in progress, may have not deemed them worthy of preservation.

# 7 : Cross staff

## 1342

The cross staff, or Jacob's staff, preceded the astrolabe and sextant as a method for determining latitude and maintaining a course along a line of latitude, which is known as latitude sailing. European navigators used it extensively during the Age of Discovery, succeeding the Kamal, used by Arab navigators since the time of Sinbad.

Made of wood, the cross staff measures the angle between the horizon and a celestial body by moving the scale along the staff until both are aligned on opposite sides of the vane. This proved difficult to do from the deck of a moving vessel, and the cross staff was eventually replaced by the backstaff.

Captain John Davis invented his version of the backstaff in 1594 in an effort to improve the cross staff's accuracy when used at sea. His first quadrant staff had an arc that slid along the staff. The navigator looked along the staff and observed the horizon through a slit in the horizon vane. By sliding the arc so that the shadow aligned with the horizon,

the angle of the Sun was then read on the graduated staff. The accuracy of the instrument was largely down to the length of the staff, and the larger ones were found to be too unwieldy.

For his second design, Davis placed the shadow vane on a transom, which could be moved along a graduated scale to indicate the angle of the shadow above the staff. This instrument was perfected in the mid-1600s when the quadrant arc was split into two parts and a smaller radius arc, with a span of 60 degrees, was mounted above the staff with a second arc, with a span of 30 degrees, mounted below. A moveable sight vane was mounted on the lower arc, thus giving the navigator the ability to accurately align two line segments. This became known as the English backstaff.

In a later modification the shadow vane was replaced by a Flamsteed glass lens, which was able to project a much brighter image of the Sun onto the horizon vane.

An illustration of a Jacob's staff in use, taken from
John Sellers' *Practical Navigation*, published in 1672.

# 8 : Porthole

## 1490

Portholes are essentially just round windows, so they may not seem much of a milestone in the history of sailing. But the technology needed to cut a large hole in the side of a boat and then seal it to prevent any water ingress is so demanding that no one tried it for several thousand years. Indeed, so deep-rooted was the fear of springing a leak that most sailors vehemently resisted any attempt to cut holes in the sides of their boats – that is, until they needed to win a war.

It was developments in cannon design that led to the invention of the first portholes (or gun ports). Ships had been fitted with artillery since the beginning of the 14th century, but this usually consisted of small calibre weapons mounted on the fore and aft castle of the craft, which had only limited use, since the primary battle tactic was still for military personnel to board an enemy ship and engage in hand-to-hand combat.

As large cannon began to dominate land battles, it became clear that they could play a similar role at sea. But to carry the weight of such large weapons without the ship becoming top heavy, cannon had to be placed low down, and that meant cutting holes in (or 'piercing') the sides of the ship in order to create a space through which the cannons could fire.

There are many different theories about who invented the gun port. The French claim it was a boatbuilder from Brest, François Descharges, who fitted them to Henry VIII's warship *Henry Grace à Dieu* in 1515. The Portuguese say King John II came up with the idea when he fitted his caravels with heavy cannon in 1490. Other evidence suggests they may have been in existence at the Siege of Rhodes in 1480. Most probably, like other timely inventions, they were developed simultaneously in several countries. In any case, by the 1520s, gun ports were in general use and it would be only several decades before the horrific destruction inflicted by 'line of battle' tactics – where ships literally lined up to fire broadsides at each other – would become the dominant strategy in naval warfare.

Not that gun ports were without their problems. The *Mary Rose* (page 30) and the *Vasa* (page 36) were just two of the better-known ships sunk when a sudden wind heeled them over, causing water to come flooding in through their open ports.

Once the concept of piercing a hull for guns had been accepted, it was a small step to cutting holes for ventilation and light. And so the porthole was invented. The term is thought to originate from the French word *porte*, meaning 'door', which was corrupted into 'porthole'. Unlike the original gun ports, most portholes are round, creating a stronger structure less prone to rot.

So ubiquitous are portholes today, it is hard to imagine a picture of a boat without a little line of circles inscribed on the hull.

A brass-rimmed porthole set into the side of a
wooden yacht. The opening mechanism is designed
to provide a tight seal so that it does not let in water
when the vessel is at sea.

# 9 : Hammock

## 1492

Everyone knows a true sailor sleeps in a hammock – it's part of the iconography of the sea. And yet hammocks were only introduced to Europe little more than 500 years ago. Before that, sailors slept in bunks or on the deck, sometimes suffering broken bones as a result.

It was the Mayans of Central America who probably invented hammocks some 1,000 years ago. They constructed their hammocks with the bark of the hamak tree, although the more plentiful sisal (also used for making rope and which could be softened by rubbing) gradually replaced it. Sleeping in a hammock made sense in a tropical climate, as the web-like contraption was well ventilated and raised the sleeper above the ground, clear of dangerous insects, snakes and other marauding animals. The practice soon spread from Central to South America and the neighbouring Caribbean.

When Christopher Columbus returned to Europe after 'discovering' the New World in 1492, he didn't bring back spices and gold, as he had promised, but he did bring back pineapples, turkeys, tobacco – and hammocks. Soon after, the Spanish writer Gonzalo Fernández de Oviedo y Valdés (otherwise known as 'Oviedo') travelled to the Caribbean and spent 30 years recording the indigenous cultures, including the locals' sleeping arrangements: 'The Indians sleep in a bed they call an "hamaca", which looks like a piece of cloth with both an open and tight weave, like a net ... made of cotton ... about 2.5 or 3 yards long, with many henequen twine strings at either end which can be hung at any height. They are good beds, and clean ... and since the weather is warm they require no covers at all ... and they are portable so a child can carry it over the arm.' European colonisers quickly took to the 'hamaca', and by 1570 it was already in widespread use among South American settlers.

Hammocks turned out to be very practical aboard ship, too, as they took up less space than traditional bunks and could be folded out of the way when not in use. What's more, they stayed more or less upright as the ship rolled, reducing the effects of seasickness and preventing sailors being thrown out of their bunks. In 1597, the Royal Navy formally adopted hammocks. Unlike the Caribbean version, however, the Navy's hammock was made of solid canvas, and could become sweaty and claustrophobic in hot weather – especially when slung 14in (35cm) apart, as Navy regulations stipulated. Despite this limitation, hammocks remained virtually unchanged and the Navy used them right into the 1950s. Hammocks are still popular on board pleasure vessels, though today they are more commonly used for siestas and sunbathing – usually strung out between the mast and the forestay – while a comfy bunk below decks is now relied on to ensure a good night's sleep.

An engraving from *Le Journal de la Jeunesse* (Paris 1870) showing cadets at the École Navale, the French Naval Academy, in the hammocks in which they slept, clearly preparing them for life at sea.

# 10 : Mary Rose

## 1511

When Henry VIII became King of England in 1509, he inherited a small navy and crumbling coastal fortifications. Alarmed by the constant threat of war with France to the south and Scotland to the north, the young king threw himself into rebuilding England's sea defences. He restored old forts, built new ones and established efficient foundries to produce an inexhaustible supply of cannon to defend the realm. When this wasn't enough, he imported more cannon from Belgium. He also started an unprecedented programme of shipbuilding, which laid the foundations for what would become the Royal Navy.

One of the first ships he ordered was the 500-ton (453-tonne) *Mary Rose*. Built from the wood of 600 trees (mostly oak), she was launched in Portsmouth in July 1511 and commissioned the following year. She was pressed into service at once, leading the fleet tasked with clearing the English Channel of enemy (i.e. French) ships. Her first major battle took place in August 1512 when she led an attack on 222 French ships anchored at Brest, returning home with 32 ships and 800 prisoners.

This was a period of transition in naval warfare. Up until then, the main tactic had been to board an enemy ship and engage in hand-to-hand combat. But advances in cannon design meant long-distance cannon fire was gaining favour, both on land and at sea. In order to carry the weight of such large

weapons without the ship becoming top heavy, guns had to be set low down, which only became possible with the invention of gun ports (see page 26). The *Mary Rose* encapsulates this transition. Built with a traditional clinker hull (whereby the planks overlap each other to form a watertight construction), she was rebuilt in 1536 and fitted with carvel planking (where the plank sides butt against each other and are caulked to make them waterproof), in order to allow her to carry bigger cannon.

The new armaments may have also been the cause of her undoing. On 16 July 1545, a fleet of 128 French ships entered the Solent, the stretch of water between the Isle of Wight and Portsmouth, intent on invading England. The *Mary Rose* was one of 80 English ships sent to deter the enemy. On the second day of fighting, she was caught by a sudden gust as she turned through the wind, heeling her over before her gun ports could be closed. Water rushed in through the ports and her hull quickly filled, sinking the ship in a matter of minutes and drowning most of the 700 crew. The French invasion was repelled, but at a high price.

And there the *Mary Rose* sat for more than 400 years until divers discovered her and raised her from the seabed in 1982. A massive preservation project commenced, including spraying her hull with polyethylene glycol (PEG) for 16 years to prevent it drying out, and in April 2013 the ship was

An illustration of the *Mary Rose* as depicted on the
Anthony Roll, a record of ships of the Tudor navy of the
1540s. It depicted 58 naval vessels with information on
their size, crew, armament and equipment.

displayed to the public in a brand new museum.
More than just a significant old boat, the wreck of
the *Mary Rose* yielded around 19,000 artefacts that
shed light on all aspects of Tudor life, from naval
instrument making to clothing, shoes and the
preparation of food.

# 11 : Earrings

## 1570

If there's one piece of kit every pirate worth his salt must have outside of an eye patch and bandana, it's an earring. There have been many reasons put forward for why sailors (and particularly pirates) wore earrings.

Some say they were thought to bring good luck, or at least prevent the wearer from drowning; others, that they were to be used as payment for a funeral should the wearer drown at sea and wash up in a faraway land. Some even claim that sailors etched the name of their hometown onto the earring, so that their bodies might be repatriated for burial (a kind of primitive 'dog tag', such as those worn by military personnel today), though there's no historical evidence to support this.

Another theory is that piercing the ear was thought to improve eyesight, which might seem far-fetched until you consider that acupuncturists use the pressure points in the earlobes to treat eye problems. Slightly more plausible is the idea that sailors wore earrings as badges of honour to mark major sea journeys, such as crossing the Equator or rounding Cape Horn. So the left ear was pierced on a normal west to east passage, as that was the side nearest to the Cape, while the right ear was pierced for the much tougher (being against the prevailing winds and currents) east to west rounding.

Whatever the reason, the practice probably began during Queen Elizabeth I's reign (1558–1603), which was when trade routes with Asia opened up, and European sailors were exposed to cultures where body piercing was commonplace. Asia is also the home of acupuncture, so early European adopters of the earring might well have picked up some ideas about pressure points during these visits.

Perhaps more to the point, earrings were generally in fashion in mainstream society during this time. After a spell in the doldrums during the Middle Ages, when women's headgear came down over the ears and made decorations there redundant, earrings came back in vogue during the English Renaissance. There's even an alleged portrait of Shakespeare wearing a gold earring – although some dispute whether it really is him. Sir Walter Raleigh went a step further and allowed himself to be painted wearing a large, dangly earring made of silver or mother of pearl.

Not everyone approved of course and in 1577 William Harrison wrote in outrage: 'Some lusty courtiers and gentlemen of courage do wear either rings of gold, stones or pearls in their ears whereby they imagine the workmanship of God to be not a little amended. But herein they rather disgrace than adorn their persons.'

Such disapprobation would have only encouraged many sailors, who went to sea to escape the conventions of society. If an earring gave them a roguish air, they were probably all the happier for it.

The 'Flibustiers' by Gustave Alaux depicts a group of flamboyant pirates (or filibusters) wearing earrings, along with several women in a public house on the Antilles in 1700.

# 12 : Astrolabe

## 1608

There are few more decorative and beautiful instruments than the astrolabe. With its multiple overlapping disks and intricately inscribed faces, often decorated with gold and silver, the astrolabe sometimes seems more like a work of art than a functioning mechanism – and indeed many astrolabes have spent most of their lives locked up in display cabinets instead of performing their intended task, which is of course to measure the angle of stars.

Not so the mariner's astrolabe. This was a stripped down version, reduced to its essential components – a graduated ring with an alidade (rotating arm) attached to it – and made of hefty chunks of brass to withstand the rigours of life at sea. The main body was usually cut out in the middle to reduce windage, and a heavy lump of metal was built into the lower part to make it more stable. The alidade was fitted with a pair of vanes, or sights, used to align it with the stars or Sun.

Unlike the more fancy land-borne version, which could be utilised for several other purposes including astronomy, astrology and calculating the direction of Mecca, the mariner's astrolabe was used for one thing alone: to measure the angle of the Sun or a star. This in turn enabled the mariner to work out his/her latitude (i.e. the north–south position), which was halfway to working out where they actually were.

Before a reliable method was found to calculate longitude (the east–west position), the most efficient method of navigation was to sail your ship to a known latitude and continue along that line until you reached your destination. The astrolabe was one of a number of instruments, including the quadrant and the cross staff, used to calculate latitude, and was especially popular with Portuguese sailors from the late 15th century until the 17th century, when both the sextant and the octant superseded it.

The astrolabe was relatively easy to use. A ring at the top was held in one hand, allowing the instrument to hang vertically. The alidade was then aligned with the object of interest – either by sighting the star directly through the holes in the vanes or, if the Sun was the intended navigational aid, lining up the ray of light shining through the front hole with the hole at the back. The angle was then read off the main dial and combined with the known declination of the star to give the latitude.

The advantage of the astrolabe was that it used gravity to measure the angle rather than the horizon, which meant it could be used in fog. But in rough weather, it was hard to get an accurate reading, and it was often up to 5 degrees out – an error of 300 miles (482km). Greater accuracy could be achieved with a bigger astrolabe on shore, which reduced the possible error to about half a degree, or 30 miles (48.2km) – but by then it might be too late.

This Portuguese astrolabe was made by Francisco de Goes in 1608. The angle of the Sun was measured by lining up the alidade so that a ray of sunshine passed through the hole on the upper plate onto the lower plate.

Few historic mariners' astrolabes survive, partly because they were used for just two centuries but also because they were regarded as functional instruments. They were far more likely to go down with the ship than be locked up in a display cabinet. As a result, they are more rare, and arguably more valuable, than their land-bound counterparts.

English sailor Sir Robin Knox-Johnston used a mariner's astrolabe during a solo transatlantic voyage in 1989, in order to test the navigation skills of Columbus and his crew who used the same instrument 500 years previously. From the moment he set out from the Canaries in September that year to when he reached San Salvador a month later, the Argos satellite system tracked Knox-Johnston's yacht, *Suhaili*. Remarkably, he found on arrival that he was only 12 miles (19.3km) out in his latitude calculations and 24 miles (38.6km) ahead in longitude – an overall error of less than 1 per cent over the 3,000-mile (4,828km) distance.

# 13 : *Vasa* warship

## 1628

On 10 August 1628, the 1,200-ton (10,900-metric tonne) warship *Vasa* slipped her moorings in front of the Royal Palace in Stockholm and set off on one of the most famous maiden voyages in history. As the wind was coming from the south-west, she was warped along the quayside for the first few hundred yards, after which four sails were set. The crowd cheered as the ship fired a salute and set sail for the first time. A gentle breeze pushed her across the bay, but as she emerged from under the lee of the Södermalm cliffs the wind stiffened. *Vasa* heeled to port once, twice and then, to the horror of everyone watching, slowly filled with water and sank. Her crew clung to the wreckage as boats from all around rushed to the rescue, but at least 30 of her 150 crew were trapped and killed. Sweden's most powerful ship, intended to stamp King Adolphus' authority in the region, had sunk after sailing less than 1,400 yards (1,300m).

The sinking of the *Vasa* was a heavy blow to Sweden's national pride but it was also an important lesson in naval architecture. King Adolphus ordered the ship in order to replace several vessels lost in the war with Poland and it was intended to serve as much as a statement of Swedish naval might than as an active warship. Whereas previous ships were fitted with a single cannon deck and were designed to capture ships primarily by boarding, the *Vasa* carried 64 cannon on two decks capable of firing

660lb (300kg) of shot per side, making her the most powerful ship in Scandinavia.

The trouble at that time was that the science of ship design wasn't fully understood. There was no such thing as construction drawings and ships were designed by 'rule of thumb', largely based on previous experience. The original builder of the *Vasa*, Henrik Hybertsson, had probably never built a ship with two cannon decks before and simply based the new ship on his previous designs. When he fell ill and construction was handed over to his assistant, the ship was widened by 1ft 5in (43cm), but this still wasn't enough to cope with the weight of the extra cannon deck and the resulting high sides. Worse, the aft castle was covered with elaborate carvings celebrating the wisdom of King Adolphus and mocking his enemies. Yet with every carving the builders added, they made the ship still more top heavy and ever more likely to capsize.

After her dramatic sinking, the ship lay on the seabed for more than 300 years until she was rediscovered in 1956 and raised five years later. Her subsequent restoration and conservation served as a textbook example of how such things should be done, as well as turning her into one of Sweden's top tourist attractions, attracting 29 million visitors since 1961. While the *Vasa* failed spectacularly in her original mission, 400 years later, the ship continues to inspire awe and admiration.

The meticulously restored *Vasa* shows the sheer
scale and bulk of the ship – and perhaps why she
was so vulnerable to changes in the wind.

# 14 : Barometer

## 1643

The mechanism inside a barometer is based on a vacuum and, back in the 17th century the very idea of a vacuum challenged the fundamental Christian belief in an omnipresent God. For if God was everywhere how could a vacuum (an empty space) exist? Even Aristotle supported this position with his statement that 'nature abhors a vacuum'.

This is why Italian physicist Evangelista Torricelli had to be discreet when he created a vacuum in a 32ft (9.75m) tube of water in his own house. By filling the tube with water, sealing the top and then opening the bottom in a basin of water, he observed that a certain amount of water emptied into the basin. But at a certain point, the water stopped flowing and remained in the tube, seemingly held by some mysterious force. Galileo had discussed a similar experiment and concluded that the water was held up by the 'suction' of the vacuum above. But Torricelli believed that the weight of air (atmospheric pressure) pressed down on the water in the basin and then forced it up the tube. 'We live submerged at the bottom of an ocean of air,' he wrote, 'which by unquestioned experiments is known to have weight.'

Torricelli also observed that the level of water in the tube varied from day to day, depending on the weather, thus establishing the basis of a whole new science: meteorology. He conducted the same experiment in a smaller tube using mercury, thereby creating the first barometer, which in its purest form remains unchanged to this day.

Two hundred years later, Robert Fitzroy, the former captain of *The Beagle*, was appointed as the first director of the newly formed Meteorological Office in 1854. One of his first acts was to design a simple barometer that he had manufactured and placed in harbours all around Britain to help fishermen predict the weather. The 'Fitzroy storm barometers' had weather lore rhymes inscribed on either side (e.g. 'First rise after blow foretells stronger blow') and are credited with saving hundreds of lives.

The mercury barometer was a delicate instrument, however, and it was only a matter of time before someone invented something more practical for seagoing craft. In 1844, French scientist Lucien Vidi duly devised the aneroid barometer using a thin metal disc attached to a flexible vacuum chamber. Any change in atmospheric pressure was detected by the disc and displayed on the dial through a series of levers. The levers themselves were made deliberately stiff so that the device had to be tapped to show any change, rather than move incrementally. The aneroid barometer soon became the norm (apart from meteorological stations, which still use the mercury version) and can now be found on virtually every yacht on the water, usually accompanied by a matching clock.

A plate from *Traittez des Barometres, Thermometres et Notiometres ou Hygrometres* (1688) by J D'Alence illustrating a siphon barometer in use. It shows how dampness is indicated by changes in the length of a stretched cord.

# 15 : Catamaran

## 1662

The word catamaran comes from the Tamil word *kattumaram*, which means 'tied wood'. The catamaran is a geometrically stabilised twin-hulled boat and includes 'proa canoes' stabilised with an outrigger and developed independently in Oceania, a craft that continues to carry seafaring Polynesians between remote Pacific islands.

William Dampier, a 17th-century English adventurer, observed the vessels in Malabar on the south-western coast of India. He wrote in 1697: 'They call them catamarans. These are but one log, or two, sometimes of a sort of light wood ... so small, that they carry but one man, whose legs and breech are always in the Water.'

The first documented catamaran to be built in Europe was designed by William Petty in 1662. His concept – to produce a vessel that required less wind and crew and could sail faster, and in shallower waters than contemporary monohulls – met with scepticism and was not a commercial success. Not until 1820 did Englishman Mayflower Crisp build a two-hulled merchant ship called *Original*. She was used for several years to trade during the monsoon season between Rangoon and the Tenasserim Provinces of India.

The American designer Nathanael G Herreshoff also experimented with the catamaran, launching the sailing vessel *Amaryllis* in 1876. She displayed such superior performance capabilities at her maiden regatta held off the New York Yacht Club's Staten Island station that the howls of protest from rival monohull crews led to the catamaran concept being barred from racing for another century!

The catamaran eventually gained international recognition when the two-person *Tornado* was adopted as one of the Olympic class boats in 1976. This class was dropped after the 2008 Games, and the Olympic movement has missed out on the resurgence of interest in catamarans following the adoption of wing-sailed, foil-born catamarans for the 2013 America's Cup in San Francisco, USA (won by Larry Ellison's *Oracle Team USA*).

During the 1980s, shipbuilders in Scandinavia and Australia began developing fast catamaran car ferries. The largest of these has been the HSC *Stena Voyager*, launched in 1996 to run between Belfast and Stranraer. Powered by two GE gas turbine engines, this 415ft (126.6m) catamaran could carry 375 cars and 1,500 passengers at an average speed of 40 knots, though was capable of doing 60 knots unladen. She was scrapped in 2013.

A succession of catamaran car ferries has also smashed records for fastest crossing of the Atlantic. The first to do so was the Hoverspeed *SeaCat* in 1990, which completed the 2,880-mile (4635km) distance from New York to the Lizard, Cornwall, in three days, seven hours. The current holder, *Cat-Link V* (former name), crossed the Atlantic in two days, twenty hours.

Terreeoboo, King of Hawaii, bringing gifts to Captain
James Cook and his crew in 1778. They travelled by
catamaran with 10 men on each side propelling it
with paddles. The engraving is from *New System of
Geography* by Thomas Bankes (London, c. 1785).

# 16 : Cat o' nine tails

## 1695

The cat o' nine tails is a multi-tailed whip once used for judicial punishment. The term first appeared in 1695, but the design is thought to be much older. The name probably originated from the fact that the nine tails inflict parallel wounds rather like a cat's claw.

The 'cat' consisted of nine knotted thongs of cotton cord, each about 2ft (76cm) long and designed to lacerate the skin, cause extreme pain and mark the victim for life. Constructed from three-strand plaited rope, the thongs were formed by unravelling the plait into three, then further unravelling each of these into three more, leaving the bearer with, of course, nine knotted thongs. Each thong had a further single knot tied at differing distances to increase the damage and pain. All the chords were seized to a thicker rope that served as the handle, and the entire contraption was traditionally kept in a bag made from red baize, leading to the expression 'let the cat out of the bag'.

The naval cat, also known as the 'Captain's daughter', was ordered by Captain or court martial and administered ceremonially on deck, with the crew summoned to 'witness punishment'. A drum roll enhanced the drama, and the routine included pauses for untangling of the 'tails', and a sip of water for the victim to preserve his consciousness. After the flogging the sailor's lacerated back was rinsed with seawater, which was thought to serve as a crude antiseptic and was therefore administered to control infection. On the contrary, rather than a healing salve, it merely caused the sailor to endure additional pain, giving rise to the expression 'rubbing salt into his wounds', a vindictive way of increasing the injury already imposed.

A bosun's mate usually made a new cat for each flogging, though in Nelson's day the condemned sailor was invariably awarded the task, to be completed while he sat in irons during the 24-hour prelude to his punishment. Extra lashings were administered if his ropework was found to be sub-standard. Each lash could be administered by a fresh bosun's mate and came from both left and right sides to criss-cross the weals and produce maximum pain.

This form of punishment ceased in 1881.

A 19th century wood engraving showing a British sailor, tied
to the ship's grating, being flogged with cat o' nine-tails.

# 17 : Jolly Roger

## 1700

Go into any crowded anchorage in summer and chances are you'll find a boat teeming with children flying the Jolly Roger. The flag, with its instantly recognisable skull and crossbones against a black background, has become associated with a certain kind of cheeky, fun-loving, sociable family fun. Flying a Jolly Roger tells everyone you don't take life too seriously and are generally 'up for a laugh'. How different to 300 years ago. Back then, the sight of a Jolly Roger flown from a ship's mast would have filled you with the fear of imminent death, for pirates were a widespread threat, and their morbid flags were not a laughing matter.

The so-called Golden Age of Piracy (c. 1650–1725) was mainly concentrated on the Caribbean trade routes, where sailing ships carried rich cargoes from the New World to the Old. The area was relatively un-policed, there was a great deal of loot passing through it, and there were countless bays and anchorages in which pirate ships could 'vanish'. In 1716, after the end of the Spanish War in Europe, there were also plenty of laid-off seamen and former privateers with unwanted skills and no social security to fall back on. A life of adventure beckoned.

Far from receiving the scorn they justly deserved, these pirates seem to have caught the public imagination from the outset, and quickly became folklore heroes. Tales of the derring-do of such violent characters as Henry Morgan, Captain Kidd, 'Calico' Jack Rackham, Edward 'Blackbeard' Teach and Bartholomew 'Black Bart' Roberts soon slipped into legend and have remained there ever since. A symbol of the hero status they enjoyed is the 'house flags', or Jolly Rogers, they created for themselves.

One of the earliest references to the Jolly Roger was in July 1700, when the HMS *Poole* chased a pirate ship off the Cape Verde Islands and her captain described the 'cross bones, death's head and an hour glass' on the ship's flag. Charles Johnson in his *A General History of the Pyrates*, published in 1724, also used the term 'Jolly Roger', although there is no mention of the notorious skull and crossbones, suggesting the expression was already a common term for pirate flags in general, which exhibited a variety of designs, including skeletons, bleeding hearts, hourglasses (signifying 'your time is up'!), cutlasses and, of course, the skull and crossbones. The backgrounds were either black (for death) or red (for blood), with motifs in white, red or black.

Bartholomew Roberts had two flags: the first depicted Bartholomew and the devil holding an hour glass (presumably suggesting it was both he and the devil who decided when your time was up), the second showing him standing on two skulls, representing the Barbadians and the Martinicans, against whom he apparently held a grudge.

But why would a pirate want to advertise his presence anyway? Certainly in the first phase of an

Usually seen flying as part of a re-enactment today, it's
hard to imagine the dread that a Jolly Roger would have
engendered in another ship three centuries ago.

attack it would benefit a marauder to conceal his
identity, and this is exactly what they did: initially,
they would fly either no flags or false flags in order
to fool their victim. Once their target was within
reach, they then raised the Jolly Roger with the
express intention of alarming the enemy's crew into
submission. A black Jolly Roger meant surrender
now, and your life might be saved. If that was
ignored, a red flag was raised, meaning no mercy
would be shown. At that point, you knew you were
in serious trouble. In other words, these were the
tactics of shock and awe, 300 years before their time.

# 18 : Ship's wheel

## 1703

The ship's wheel was one of the most significant mechanical improvements to ship design during the 18th century, and a great advance on the whip staff that preceded it. The invention of the ship's wheel is credited to the Royal Navy thanks to photographs of ship models from that period, but there is no hard evidence to support this. What is clear is that the ship's wheel did not become commonplace until around 1715.

Early wheels were sited behind the mizzenmast, which obstructed the helmsman's view. They were designed to have two men operating them during heavy weather, although the small amount of space around the wheel caused the sailors to get in each other's way. It wasn't until 1740 that ships were fitted with two wheels on a single spindle at either end of a drum winch, which allowed four men to steer when conditions were bad.

These first wheel systems suffered from a lack of equal amounts of tension when the ropes were at their extremity, making steering something of an imprecise art. This flaw remained for 70 years until a man named Pollard, the master boatbuilder at Portsmouth Dockyard, introduced 'sweeps and rowles' into the system. This new system was tested by Captain Bentinck in 1771 and proved such a success that it became the standard on all Royal Navy ships by 1775.

A traditional ship's wheel is composed of eight cylindrical wooden spokes shaped like balusters, each joined at a central wooden hub, or nave, which houses the axle. The square hole at the centre of the hub is a 'drive square', and is often lined with a brass that carries the name of the manufacturer. The outer rim is composed of four sections each made up of stacks of three felloes: the facing felloe, the middle felloe and the after felloe. Each group of three felloes makes up a quarter of the distance around the rim. Each spoke runs through the middle felloe creating a series of handles on the outside of the wheel's rim. One of these spokes, the king spoke, was frequently given extra grooves at its tip or fancy rope work around its length, so that a helmsman steering in the dark could determine the exact position of the rudder by feel alone (when the king spoke is pointed straight up, the rudder is also straight).

A traditional ship's wheel, of polished wood with
brass trimmings on a sailing ship

# 19 : Neva Yacht Club
# – the world's first yacht club

## 1718

Tsar Peter the Great of Russia was keenly interested in shipbuilding and sailing throughout his life. As a young man he spent time incognito as an apprentice in a shipyard in the Netherlands in order to learn about the Dutch merchant fleet and the technology behind their ships. In order to continue with his passion, on 12 April 1718 he founded the Neva Yacht Club on the eponymous river in St Petersburg. He provided a fleet of 141 small ships with which to entertain his family and members, the Russian nobility and, perhaps unwittingly, created the first version of a model wherein sailors convened to sail for pleasure. He also instigated the club burgee – a version of the Russian Navy Ensign.

The initial version of the club, so closely associated with Peter the Great, closed following the death of the Tsar and the loss of his personal sponsorship. However, in 1892, in memory of Peter the Great's 'Nevsky Flot', the Neva Yacht Club was revived by a group of highly ranked officers serving in the Russian Imperial Navy. This version of the club organised regattas for large cruising yachts for the next 25 years until it too was disbanded once again, this time after the Russian Revolution. The current Neva Yacht Club was re-established in 1958.

If longevity is the marker, the sailing club with a serious claim to being the oldest still in existence was founded in Ireland just two years after the Neva. William O'Brien, the Ninth Lord Inchiquin, and five of his friends set up the Water Club of Cork Harbour (better known now as the Royal Cork Yacht Club) in 1720, and it is still operating today, nearly 300 years later. Initially, club sailing activities involved sailing in formation, copying the manoeuvres of contemporary navies. Sailors communicated using different flags and firing cannons and the club still possesses paintings dating from 1738 that show club yachts carrying out such manoeuvres.

Peter I, the Great (1672–1725), Tsar of Russia is seen here dressed as a ship's carpenter's apprentice so that he could go incognito while studying the art of shipbuilding, which he did at Amsterdam and Deptford on a tour of western Europe in 1698–1699.

# 20 : Grog

## 1740

Sailing a square-rigger, with its endless sails to hoist and decks to scrub, was thirsty work. To prevent the crew from dehydrating, ships had to carry hundreds of barrels of water, along with a daily issue of alcohol, usually in the form of beer. Indeed, 16th-century sailors regarded their gallon of beer as a daily right rather than a privilege, and the Admiralty even had to set up its own breweries to cope with the demand.

As ships started to venture further afield, however, the beer tended to go off and, as the Lord High Admiral Charles Howard noted in 1588, 'nothing doth displease the seaman so as to sour beer'. Wine was sometimes used as a substitute, and in 1650, Admiral Robert Blake issued watered-down brandy instead of beer. But the Admiralty couldn't always count on plentiful supplies of Spanish brandy and/or French wine, since England was invariably at war with either France or Spain, and sometimes both.

In 1740, the British Vice Admiral Edward Vernon introduced a beverage that comprised a combination of water or weak beer and a citrus juice – invariably lemon or lime – to dilute a ration of rum. It seems that the juice was added to stop the drink from going off, but that it was later found to have the added benefit of helping to prevent scurvy, a painful and debilitating disease caused by lack of vitamin C.

Admiral Vernon was known for his wearing of coats made from 'grogram' or grosgrain fabric, a loosely woven mix of silk and wool or mohair which had given him the name 'Old Grog'. This nickname soon came to apply to the drink that he had unwittingly created.

Drunken customers at the grog shop from a cartoon
sequence known as *The Drunkard's Progress, or
the direct road to poverty, wretchedness & ruin*
by John Warner Barber, 1798–1885.

# 21 : Scrimshaw

## 1745

Scrimshaw is the elaborate engraving and scrollwork that whalers add to the bones of their catch and the tusks of walruses. Whalers working the Pacific Ocean from around 1745 created scrimshaw, and continued until an international ban on commercial whaling was instigated in 1973. The craft now survives as a hobby, and many pieces have considerable value as collectables.

Scrimshaw was a way to help pass the time when whalers were unable to work at night. Early scrimshaw was carved using sailing needles and the etchings were coloured with candle black, soot, tobacco juice or ink, bought by the sailors before the voyage. Their subjects were almost inevitably maritime in theme and included the whales they hunted as well as the processes of whaling and portraits of the artist's fellow whalers. Though the most skilled artist might carve from life, many relied on pre-existing illustrations for their patterns. The items they carved ranged from the practical (including knife handles, spoons and games) to the purely artistic and decorative.

Scrimshaw crafted before 1973 on sperm whale and walrus ivory can be bought or sold legally as can art created from walrus tusks bearing the Alaska State walrus ivory registration tag, and post-law walrus ivory that has been scrimshawed by a native Alaskan Indian or Eskimo.

Scrimshanders and collectors continue to acquire legal whale teeth and marine tusks through estate sales and auctions, but must always check the bone's provenance with care. Customs officials worldwide can seize bones that they find to have been sourced illegally.

A modern work of scrimshaw by artist Michael J Vienneau reflects the seafaring history of this very particular art form.

WHALING BARK
CHARLES W. MORGAN

# 22 : Naval uniforms

## 1748

Lord Anson first brought officer uniforms into use in the Royal Navy in 1748 under Naval Uniform Regulations, as a method of recognition for being 'in the service of the Crown'. The 'best uniform' – an embroidered blue coat with white facings, worn unbuttoned with white breeches and stockings – was worn for ceremonial occasions. A simpler 'working rig' had less embroidery and was therefore worn every day. The distinctive midshipman's white collar patch first appeared in 1758.

The 'best uniform' remained in use until 1767, when the working rig replaced it and a simpler 'undress' uniform was then introduced as a replacement for everyday use. In the period of the French Revolutionary Wars, a plain blue 'undress' coat was introduced for everyday use, with epaulettes introduced in 1795. Strips of lace around the cuffs to distinguish the different ranks of admiral also appeared in the same year, and officers wore their rank insignia, as stripes around the cuff, with a curl in the top stripe, from 1856.

The Admiralty first established uniforms for lower ranks in 1857, in order to replace the 'slops', or ready-made clothing, sold to the ship's crew by a contractor. Captains had invariably set general standards of appearance for seamen on their vessels, but until the mid-1850s there had been little uniformity between ships' crews. For example, in 1853, the commanding officer of HMS *Harlequin* paid for his crew to dress as the Harlequin (a comic servant-character made famous in the Italian *Commedia dell'arte* form of theatre), which probably contributed to the Admiralty's decision to adopt a standard uniform.

In 1825, trousers replaced white breeches, although the practice of wearing white trousers with naval uniforms continued for officers serving overseas until 1939. In 1877, a white tunic and trousers were introduced for those serving in the Tropics. During the Second World War, a blue working dress was approved, and caps were given white tops for year-round use. Blue caps were abolished in 1956.

Other changes to the standard uniform notably include the removal of the blue jacket in 1890, and the replacement of bell-bottoms with flared trousers in 1977. In 1997, the Admiralty introduced a standardisation programme and now all ratings – both male and female – wear the same ceremonial uniform.

Royal Navy uniforms have also served as the template for navies in other countries, especially those within the British Commonwealth. Modern uniforms of the Royal Australian Navy and Royal New Zealand Navy are virtually identical to Royal Navy uniforms, with the exception of nationality flashes at shoulder height and on rank slides. The Chilean Navy, which is modelled on British practices, has also adopted similar uniforms across all ranks.

Aquatints of a midshipman (left) and a lieutenant
(right) from 1799, showing the more formal dress of
the higher ranked officer, complete with trimmed
facings, breeches and stockings.

# 23 : *The Female Soldier*
# by Hannah Snell

1750

Female sailors are now a regular sight aboard warships, but back in 1750 the rule among most menfolk was 'to keep 'em barefoot and pregnant'. Heaven help anyone who made that suggestion to Hannah Snell, who signed up as a Royal Marine in 1748 and successfully concealed her gender for two years. She only revealed her true identity during a drinking session with crewmates at a London pub on 2 June 1750, where she proclaimed: 'Why gentlemen, James Gray will cast off his skin like a snake and become a new creature. In a word, gentlemen, I am as much a woman as my mother ever was and my real name is Hannah Snell.'

Snell had sailed to India, fought in mud-filled trenches at the siege of Pondicherry and been severely wounded in battle (though one wonders at the standard of nursing in those times that no one twigged her disguise). Once Hannah's shipmates had recovered from their shock discovery, they encouraged her to capitalise on her extraordinary story, suggesting that she request a pension from the Duke of Cumberland, then head of the English Army. Hannah followed their advice and approached the duke two weeks later while he was reviewing troops in St James's Park. Surprised by the curious figure before him, the duke accepted the petition that detailed her many adventures.

Within days, news of Hannah's exploits had reached the press and the public clamoured for more information. Keen to profit from this notoriety, she sold her story to a London publisher who published it under the title *The Female Soldier*, and began to make appearances on stage. In November 1750, the Royal Chelsea Hospital recognised Snell's military service and gave her a lifetime pension. Hannah lived for another 40 years, marrying twice and raising two sons. In 1791, she was admitted to a lunatic asylum where she died six months later.

Hannah Snell pictured on the battlefield in the dress of a soldier. The image is said to have been 'drawn from life' although she stands away from the violence that is going on around her.

# 24 : Royal Hospital Haslar
## – first naval hospital

### 1753

Founded during the reign of King George I, the Royal Hospital Haslar in Gosport, Hampshire, was the country's foremost and ultimately the last of Britain's military hospitals. Designed by Theodore Jacobsen, this Royal Navy facility was not only the biggest hospital in the UK but was also the largest brick building of its day. Opened in 1753, the hospital had a long and distinguished history in the medical care of service personnel until falling victim to military budget cuts in 2009, when the site was sold for redevelopment.

Among the many medical breakthroughs made by leading physicians attached to the hospital was a cure for scurvy. The hospital also housed the country's first blood bank to treat wounded soldiers during the Second World War, and had several notable specialist medical facilities, including a decompression chamber and a zymotic isolation ward, together with an asylum to treat sailors with psychiatric disorders.

In 1902, the hospital was renamed the Royal Naval Hospital Haslar and in 1966, its remit was extended to cover all three services when the unit was renamed the Royal Military Hospital Haslar. Thirty years on, and the hospital went back to its original name, Royal Hospital Haslar, when its management was transferred to the local NHS Trust.

The military Royal Hospital Haslar, Gosport,
Hampshire, pictured c. 1840 showing its position on
the Stoke Lake. The engraving is by J & F Harwood.

# 25 : Sextant

## 1757

The sextant is a navigation instrument designed to measure the altitude of celestial bodies in order to determine a vessel's latitude and longitude. It was derived from the octant, invented at the turn of the 18th century by English inventor John Bird. He produced the first sextant in 1757, after Admiral John Campbell found the octant wanting when it came to measuring lunar distances. The 90-degree angle subtended by the arc of the instrument was insufficient to measure some of the larger angular distances required and so he suggested that the angle be increased to 120 degrees, or one-sixth of a circle – hence the name sextant.

The wooden-framed octant became obsolete as instrument makers worked to develop the sextant using more advanced materials and techniques. Early brass models were heavy, which led to some handshaking as navigators strained to hold the instrument up to their eye. This flaw in the design

was overcome in 1788, when Edward Troughton introduced the double-framed sextant. This utilised two frames held in parallel about a centimetre apart, which significantly increased the stiffness of the frame and allowed for a lighter construction.

Troughton also experimented with alternative materials, plating the scales with silver, gold and platinum to minimise corrosion. Modern sextants are now mass-produced in precision-made plastic, in order to make them lighter and more affordable.

The sextant remained in everyday use and was used to measure noon, Sun and other celestial sights in order to determine positions of latitude and longitude until the advent of early GPS systems in the 1980s. It could also be used to great effect to sight the height of a landmark and give a measure of distance off. Held horizontally, it could be used to measure the angle between two fixed objects to obtain a position on a chart.

A young midshipman pictured c.1799 carrying a sextant, which would have have been trained to use for navigating. The print is an aquatint made by Thomas Rowlandson (1756–1827).

# 26 : Square plates

## 1758

Square plates, usually with a raised edge or a scooped-out centre to prevent the food from slipping off, were known as 'trenchers'. Sailors used them throughout the 18th century as they were apparently easier to handle in a rough sea and much less likely to slip off the table. Square plates have been found on various wrecks, including that of HMS *Invincible*, which foundered in the Solent in 1758.

The phrase 'three square meals a day' is said to stem from the time when every sailor in the Royal Navy was issued with a square wooden plate. While basic rations would fill only the round hollow, a more substantial portion would fill the square section as well, so a sailor getting a hearty ration could be said to be getting his 'three square meals'.

Certainly the plates exist, but the provenance of the phrase is less plausible for there is no evidence of this tale in any Royal Navy records or ships' logs. Instead, it is seen as one of the best-known examples of folk-etymology. The phrase exists, the square plates exist, but then someone invents a plausible story to fit – it is almost certainly a case of two and two making five.

The 'square' phrase, meaning 'wholesome' or 'fulsome', is of US origin and dates back to the 1850s, a century after the wooden plates were in use on Royal Navy ships. However, there is one phrase that can be said to originate from the plates' edges, known as 'fiddles': it is said that a sailor who took more than his basic food ration would be 'on the fiddle'.

The square plate had a carved channel to stop food from
slipping off the plate when conditions at sea were choppy.

# 27 : Lloyd's Register

## 1760

The idea of organising a register of shipping came about in 1760 over a cup of coffee. Edward Lloyd's Coffee House in Lombard Street, London, was a haunt of merchants and insurance underwriters, and it was they who decided to record information on the condition of vessels, rather than rely on the often-rosy picture painted by ship owners.

Lloyd's Register became the world's first classification society, rating vessels after a survey of the condition of their hulls and equipment. Then in 1768, the society introduced the A1 standard to indicate a ship of the highest class, and this symbol of quality remains to this day.

The 19th century brought huge changes in seafaring, as steam superseded sail, and timber gave way to iron and steel, ushering in ships of unprecedented size. Lloyd's Register met these challenges, formulating construction and best practice guidelines based on practical experience. The organisation rapidly earned respect around the world, and began to appoint surveyors abroad, the first going to Newfoundland in 1812 to oversee construction for British ship owners. Further appointments were made during the 1860s across Europe, India, Australia and Hong Kong, and by the early 1880s, Lloyd's Register classed almost half of the world's shipping.

As shipbuilding became more complex, Lloyd's Register extended its classification to cover the testing of anchors and cables, together with the quality of iron and steel, and began to expand into non-marine areas, starting with refrigerated cold stores for the Port of London Authority in 1911.

The First World War brought further opportunities, and Lloyd's Register surveyors began evaluating shell steel for the French government and copper pipes produced for American shipbuilders. Experience in many sectors led to work with the power generation, oil and gas sectors from the 1930s, and the nuclear industry from 1953 with the proposed atomic power station at Calder Hall in the north of England

Lloyd's Register still has a base in London and with many other offices around the world. As a global engineering, technical and business services organisation it operates across many industry sectors.

A cartoon showing an early Lloyd's surveyor
supposedly checking the condition of a very decrepit
boat. The ships they came to inspect would have
been on a far grander scale than this one.

# 28 : Cork lifejacket (UK)

## 1765

Back in the mid-18th century, the number of British seamen who drowned each year was in its thousands. One estimate put the figure at 4,200 annually, a quarter of whom could have been saved had they been wearing a flotation device. Those figures prompted Dr John Wilkinson to design and patent the first lifejacket using cork as the buoyancy material.

To promote his invention, Wilkinson wrote a book, *Tutamen Nauticum: or the Seaman's Preservation from Shipwreck, Diseases and Other Calamities*, and in a message aimed at penny-pinching ship owners, wrote that his lifejacket would save men from perishing 'with the greatest ease and certainty at a charge not worth notice'.

In 1854, the Royal National Lifeboat Institution (RNLI) Inspector Captain John Ward created the next generation of cork lifejacket. The vest-style jacket consisted of small blocks of cork sewn onto canvas, which allowed sufficient freedom for rowing or swimming. To encourage merchant vessels to carry lifejackets for crew, the RNLI sold them at low prices, arguing that 'the value of these simple and inexpensive instruments has been proved in too many cases to need any argument in their favour'.

If further proof of the jacket's worth was needed, it came in 1861 when the Whitby lifeboat capsized. Henry Freeman, the youngest aboard, was the only crewman to be wearing the new-style cork lifejacket. The remaining 13 men all perished.

Cork lifejackets remained a popular choice for the rest of the century until a new design using kapok, 'a soft, fibrous vegetable material', was introduced in 1904. Early designs proved too bulky to both store and wear, so it took more than a decade for the cork jackets to be phased out. Passengers aboard the *Titanic* in 1912, for instance, wore a modified version of Ward's cork jacket, and the subsequent enquiry into her sinking showed that the solidity of the cork actually broke the jaws of some people and rendered others unconscious after they had jumped into the water.

Although cork had started to be overtaken by other materials, in the early years of the 20th century, this lifeboatman, from Filey in North Yorkshire, UK, shown wearing a cork lifejacket in around 1920.

# 29 : Tattoos

## 1769

Tattooing has been a skilled art since Neolithic times. The oldest tattooed human skin was found on the upper lip of a Chinchorro culture mummy, from South America dating back to the sixth millennium BC. The oldest evidence of the art in Europe is on the body of Ötzi the Iceman, dating from the late fourth millennium BC. His body is covered with 61 tattoos in the form of groups of lines or crosses, produced by fine incisions into which charcoal was rubbed. Most of Ötzi's tattoos are on parts of his body that must have caused him pain during his lifetime and many of the tattooed areas correspond to modern acupuncture lines.

The art has long been associated with sailors, ever since the time Britain's maritime fleet began making contact with non-European cultures. During a voyage in 1577 to find a north-west passage to China and it's promise of gold, three ships and 120 men under the command of Sir Martin Frobisher took prisoner a native Inuit man, woman and child. The woman had tattoos on her chin and forehead and, on their return to England, she became a great attraction at the court of Elizabeth I. Sadly, all three Inuits died within a month.

In the 17th century, it became usual practice for British pilgrims to be tattooed in order to commemorate their voyages to the Holy Lands. In 1691, William Dampier brought a native who had a tattooed body from the western part of New Guinea to London. He was then displayed as a freak at vaudeville shows and became known as the 'Painted Prince'.

Captain James Cook made three voyages to the South Pacific between 1766 and 1779, and returned home with tales of 'tattooed savages'. It was then that the word 'tattoo', which comes from the Tahitian *tatau*, was first introduced into the English language. Cook first noted his observations regarding these types of body modifications in the log of HMS *Endeavour* while at anchor in Tahiti in July 1769: 'Both sexes paint their Bodys, Tattow, as it is called in their Language. This is done by inlaying the Colour of Black under their skins, in such a manner as to be indelible ... This method of Tattowing I shall now describe ... As this is a painful operation, especially the Tattowing of their Buttocks, it is performed but once in their Lifetimes.'

Sir Joseph Banks, Cook's science officer and expedition botanist, returned to England with his own tattoo. Banks was a regarded member of the English aristocracy and had bought his position with Cook in order to join the expedition. In turn, Cook returned with a tattooed Raiatean man named Omai, who he presented to King George III and the English Court. Many of Cook's ordinary seamen also came back with tattoos, starting a tradition that would soon become synonymous with sailors and spread rapidly to seaports around the globe.

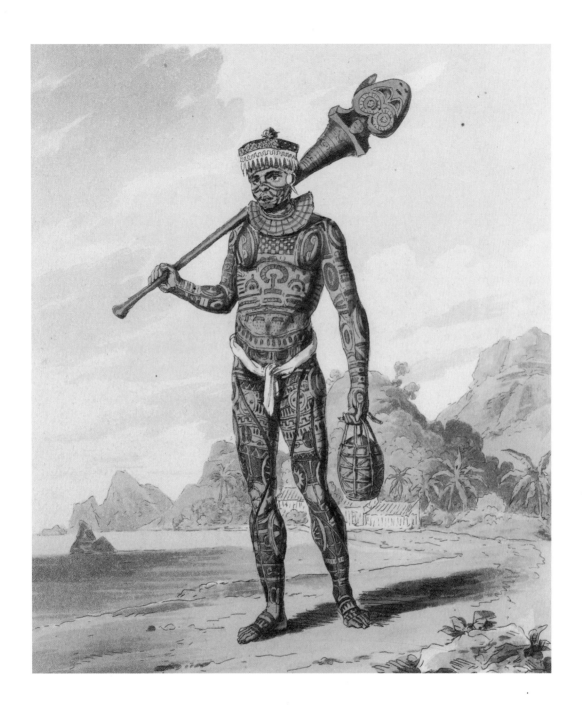

An etching by J A Atkinson after his own drawing, of a tattooed Polynesian man, from Nukahiwa (now Nuku Hiva in French Polynesia). The German seafarer Ivan Fedorovich Kruzenshtern (1770–1846) arrived there in May 1804 and traded with its inhabitants and this image was the frontispiece to his *Voyage Around the World*.

# 30 : Harrison's marine chronometer

## 1775

Longitude is a geographic coordinate that specifies the east-west position of a point on the Earth's surface. A series of meridians – lines running from the North to the South Poles – connect places of the same longitude. While latitude could be quite simply measured using a quadrant or astrolabe, the question of how to measure longitude was a problem that confounded many of the best scientists and mathematicians prior to the 18th century.

In the search for the New World, the quest to calculate any point of longitude with a degree of accuracy at sea had become one of such importance that in 1714, the British government offered a £20,000 prize for a solution that could provide longitude to within half a degree or two minutes of time. Proposals came from far and wide, and included suggestions for squaring the circle and inventing a perpetual motion machine. Before long, 'finding the longitude' became a catchphrase for the pursuits of fools and lunatics. Many believed that the problem could not be solved.

But, indeed, there was a solution, and it lay in producing an accurate clock that would be impervious to motion, and changes in humidity or temperature, at the reference place. Although the Flat Earth Society still existed to cast doubts about the globe's curvature, it was generally accepted at this time that the world was round, and that for every 15 minutes one was to travel eastward, the local time moved one hour ahead; likewise, travelling west, the local time moved back one hour for every 15 minutes of longitude.

Sailors could already measure local time by observing the Sun, but navigation required that they also knew the time at that same moment at some reference point, such as the 0-degree Greenwich Meridian, in order to calculate their longitude. Alternatively, astronomy could be used to find the reference time, and in 1675, King Charles II founded the Royal Observatory with this in mind. He reckoned that if an accurate catalogue of the positions of the stars could be made, and the position of the Moon relative to the stars then measured, the Moon's motion could be used as a natural clock to calculate Greenwich Mean Time. Sailors at sea could measure the Moon's position relative to bright stars, or use tables that presented the Moon's position, compiled at the Royal Observatory, to calculate the time at Greenwich. This means of finding longitude was known as the 'Lunar Distance Method'.

The longitude problem was eventually solved in the mid-18th century, by a carpenter from Lincolnshire with little formal education. John Harrison took on the scientific and academic establishment, and through extraordinary mechanical insight, talent and determination, he won the Longitude Prize.

Detail of an oil painting by Thomas King of
John Harrison (1693–1776) with the marine
chronometer which he invented.

John Harrison built his first longcase clock
entirely from wood in 1713, aged just 20. Then,
working with his younger brother, James, they
produced a revolutionary turret clock for the stables
at Brocklesby Park, seat of the Pelham family. At the
time, oils were poorly refined and one of the major

causes of failure in clocks. Harrison's clock was
revolutionary because it required no lubrication. It
was radical thinking like this that helped him to
design the first accurate marine timekeeper.

Harrison completed his first marine chronometer,
H1 – essentially a portable version of his precision

wooden clocks – in 1735. The moving parts were spring-controlled and counterbalanced so that, unlike a pendulum clock, H1 was independent of the force of gravity. The following year, Harrison and his timekeeper travelled to Lisbon aboard the ship *Centurion* to test the clock, and returned on the *Orford*. The clock performed well, keeping time accurately enough for Harrison to correct a misreading of the *Orford*'s longitude on the return voyage. On his arrival in England, Harrison requested financial assistance from the Commissioners of Longitude to make a second marine timekeeper.

H2 was larger and heavier but fundamentally the same design as H1. However, three years into its development, Harrison realised a major flaw in the design: the bar balances did not always counter the motion of a ship, a deficiency that could only be corrected if the balances were circular.

Harrison obtained more money from the Commissioners to work on a third timekeeper, but although H3 incorporated two new inventions – a bimetallic strip to compensate the balance spring for the effects of changes in temperature, and a caged roller bearing that became the ultimate version of Harrison's anti-friction devices – it failed to measure up to the accuracy required.

The inventor then commissioned London watchmaker John Jefferys to make him a pocket watch to his design, in order to help him with his astronomical observing and clock testing. At the time, pocket watches were not seen as serious precision timekeepers, but Harrison discovered that once certain improvements had been made, this small portable clock had the potential to be an excellent chronometer.

With more funding from the Board of Longitude, Harrison produced two watches: one small, to be worn in the pocket, and H4, Harrison's breakthrough marine chronometer. H4 is completely different to Harrison's previous timekeepers. Just 5.11in (13cm) in diameter and weighing 3.2lb (1.45kg), it looks like a very large pocket watch. On 18 November 1761, Harrison's son, William, set sail for the West Indies with H4 aboard the ship *Deptford*, and arrived in Jamaica on 19 January the following year, where the watch was found to have lost just 5.1 seconds over the course of the voyage.

The results of a second trial were even more successful. William departed for Barbados aboard the *Tartar* on 28 March 1764 and predicted the ship's arrival at Madeira with great accuracy, showing an error of just 39.2 seconds over a voyage of 47 days. This was three times better than the stipulation required in order to win the £20,000 reward.

But soon after, the goalposts for the prize were moved, with the Commissioners of Longitude insisting that they would pay half the money once

H1, the first marine timekeeper completed by John Harrison in 1735. It was his first attempt to devise a chronometer accurate enough to reliably determine a ship's longitude at sea. Harrison succeeded after building three more clocks over 24 years, culminating in H4, which won him the £20,000 prize.

Harrison had disclosed the workings of H4 to a specially appointed committee and that he allowed for copies of the watch to be made and tested. At first, Harrison refused to accept any of these conditions, but the Commissioners were equally adamant, and after several weeks, he agreed to disclose the inner workings of H4.

To qualify for the second half of the reward, Harrison had to make two more watches and have them tested. The Commissioners further insisted that he make these copies himself. Now in his late seventies, Harrison appealed to King George III and

was summoned for an interview, at which the king is said to have remarked: 'These people have been cruelly treated ... and By God, Harrison, I will see you righted!'

The king put the chronometer on trial in 1772, where it performed superbly, but the Commissioners of Longitude refused to recognise the results. In the end, the Harrisons petitioned Parliament and were finally awarded £8,750 in June 1773. Just as importantly, Harrison was finally recognised as being the first person to produce the solution that finally solved the problem of longitude.

# 31 : Daggerboard

## 1776

The daggerboard, a fully retractable centreboard used by various sailing craft, but particularly by smaller boats sailing in shallower seas, allows the boat to grip the water and prevents it from being blown in the direction of the wind. It also makes the boat more manoeuvrable and quicker to tack than a fixed keel. Daggerboards are long and thin and provide a better lift-to-drag ratio than many pivoting centreboards. They can also be very simple in design and operation, needing only to be pushed down to counter the side force that wind exerts on the sails, and pulled up whenever there is a need to navigate shallow waters.

A clay model of a junk bearing a central board found in a Chinese burial cave dating back to AD 475 suggests that the Chinese were the first civilisation to make use of a removable centreboard. The first documented use of daggerboards, however, are those fitted to a sophisticated log sailing raft used in Brazil during the 16th century.

The modern daggerboard, or drop-keel as it is sometimes called, is credited to a British seaman called Captain Schank who in 1774 designed a keel that could be raised to allow deep drafted vessels to enter harbour.

The Mirror and the Laser are two simple popular class dinghies that are fitted with a central daggerboard, but daggerboards can also be used to create vertical lift and reduce displacement on high performance craft. The best examples of this are the latest America's Cup class catamarans, which use curved or angled daggerboards as hydrofoils that enable the boats to be lifted completely clear of the water.

Using daggerboards as hydrofoils on a modern
catamaran to lift the craft clear of the water.

# 32 : Hurricane lamp

## 1780

Before François Pierre Aimé Argand invented the hurricane lamp in 1780, oil lamps were seldom very bright, smoked a great deal and the slightest breeze would extinguish the flame – a particularly irritating problem on board ship. The son of a Swiss watchmaker, Argand was a scientist with a particular interest in chemistry. His hurricane lamp is perhaps one of the most enduring designs ever and still produced by the million over two centuries later, almost invariably in a form that its inventor would still recognise.

Argand realised that a cylindrical wick that allowed air to flow both through and around itself would produce a brighter light than a conventional wick. The glass chimney he set over the wick protected the flame from wind gusts, while the control nob enabled the user to adjust the height of the wick and control the strength of light produced. Whale or olive oil acted as fuel, although today paraffin is the preferred accelerant.

Piracy, sea battles and transoceanic voyages were part and parcel of life in the 18th and 19th centuries, and mariners quickly adapted the wind-resistant hurricane lamp for use on their vessels. Hurricane lamps became necessary equipment for ships and in addition to lighting cabins and decks, were used as anchor lamps and to send signals from ship to ship.

The hurricane lamp has scarcely changed in form

since it was first invented in the late 18th century.

# 33 : Ship in a bottle

## 1784

Sometimes extraordinary in their detail, to the uninitiated, multi-masted sailing ships contained in narrow-necked bottles remain both a maritime cliché and a conundrum in general.

The origins of the first ship in a bottle are unknown, principally because the sailors who made them to while away the hours off watch rarely signed or dated the objects. The oldest ship in a bottle with any provenance is one exhibited in the Lübeck Museum, Germany, which carries the date 1784 on a sail. The only other way to estimate age is through the bottle itself.

The origin of these 'patience bottles', as they were called, goes back to the late 16th century, when Christian scenes like that of Jesus on the cross were reproduced in bottles. During the 19th century, the construction of ship models in bottles became ever more popular and intricate, with harbour scenes even painted in as backgrounds. Made from old bones and offcuts of wood and sail thread, the sailor would construct the model with its rig laid flat on the hull, ready to be pulled up by a single thread once the ship had been inserted through the neck of the bottle.

Whatever the origin, the technique for putting ships into bottles spread to all major seafaring nations, for evidence of this art can be found in nautical museums throughout Europe, North America and Japan. In 2012, Japanese artist Yinka Shonibare created a large-scale (15.4 x 9.1ft/4.7 x 2.8m) ship-in-a bottle replica of Admiral Nelson's ship, HMS *Victory*, which sat on the fourth plinth in Trafalgar Square, as part of the rolling commission of artworks that temporarily occupy the famous site.

A seaman's craft for many years, the art of getting a
tiny ship in full sail into a bottle with a narrow neck,
is one that still has many afficionados.

# 34 : Lemon

## 1795

It is strange what small details the course of history can pivot upon. There's little doubt that the British Empire was founded on the strength of the Royal Navy, which established its global dominance in a series of battles right up to and including the Battle of Trafalgar on 21 October 1805. While it's also clear that the strength of the Royal Navy was due to economic power and political alliances, what is less clear is that it also owes its success to a surprising source: the humble lemon.

During the Age of Discovery, ships started sailing further and further afield, often for months at a time as they explored foreign lands in search of new territories, trade routes and gold. Life aboard ship was notoriously harsh: sailors were expected to work hard on meagre rations and were subjected to horrendous abuse if they failed to toe the line. But the most feared occurrence was succumbing to scurvy, caused by a deficiency of vitamin C. The symptoms of this deadly disease weren't pretty – bleeding gums, loose teeth, ulcers, skin haemorrhages, lethargy and, ultimately, death could be expected upon the outbreak of scurvy.

So devastating was the disease that it's estimated that between 1500 and 1800, it claimed the lives of some two million sailors. And nobody was immune. In 1499, Portuguese explorer Vasco da Gama lost 116 of his 170-strong crew to the disease, while in 1520 the great explorer Ferdinand Magellan lost 208 out of his 230. Indeed, up until 1795, sailors were more likely to die of scurvy than through injury in battle, drowning and all other diseases combined.

And yet the cure was available at least 200 years before it was acted upon. As early as 1593, the British explorer Sir Richard Hawkins suggested that a rather surprising cure of sour oranges and lemons were 'most fruitful for this sicknesse'. Likewise, after four months at sea, Captain James Lancaster, who led a fleet of four ships in April 1601 found that each of the ship's crews showed the usual symptoms of scurvy, that is all except the crew on his own ship. They had been served with a daily dose of lemon juice. Furthermore, in 1636, John Woodall, the so-called 'father of naval hygiene', wrote a treatise extolling the virtues of lemon juice and asserting it as a cure for the dreaded scurvy.

Each of these men had inadvertently discovered, without understanding the exact scientific explanation, that scurvy is triggered by a deficiency in vitamin C, caused by a lack of fresh fruit and vegetables in the diet while at sea. Lemons and other citrus fruit did provide a natural and easily available cure. The Admiralty ignored the evidence, preferring to believe it was mere indolence or 'foul vapours', and refusing to mollycoddle its crews with special food leaving sailors to die in their thousands.

By 1753, when the Scottish physician James Lind published the results of a controlled study on two

The ability of lemons to combat scurvy was known
for more than 200 years before the Royal Navy
finally acted on it. In the meantime, more than
two million sailors died of the disease.

groups of sailors at sea, the weight of evidence was overwhelming. But even then, it took another 42 years for the Admiralty to finally adopt lemons and limes as standard issue on naval ships. The effects were immediately apparent. By the time it came to the Battle of Trafalgar, the crews on the British ships were in much better health than their scurvy-ravaged French counterparts. And, while Nelson's unconventional battle tactics were primarily responsible for the British victory, it was healthy crews that put them into action. All thanks to the humble lemon.

# 35 : USS *Constitution*

## 1797

The USS *Constitution* is the sole remaining wooden three-masted sailing ship, built for the newly formed US Navy in 1797 following the American Declaration of Independence. As one of six identical heavy frigates authorised for construction in the Naval Act of 1794, President George Washington named the *Constitution* to mark the newly formed Constitution of the United States of America.

*Constitution* and her sisters were larger and more heavily armed than standard frigates of the period, and her first duties were to provide protection for American merchant shipping during the Quasi-War with France (1798–1800) and to defeat the Barbary pirates in the First Barbary War (1801–1805).

*Constitution* is most remembered for her actions during the War of 1812 against the British, when she captured numerous merchant ships and defeated five Royal Navy warships: HMS *Guerriere*, *Java*, *Pictou*, *Cyane* and *Levant*. The battle against *Guerriere* earned *Constitution* the nickname 'Old Ironsides', and public awareness of this event and her subsequent nickname has repeatedly saved her from facing the scrap yard. She continued to serve as

flagship in the Mediterranean and African squadrons, and completed a circumnavigation during the 1840s. During the American Civil War, she served as a training ship for the United States Naval Academy and carried US artwork and industrial displays to the Paris Exposition of 1878.

Retired from active service in 1881, *Constitution* served as a receiving ship for cadets until 1907, when she was finally designated a museum ship. She completed a three-year, 90-port tour of the United States in 1934 and sailed again, first to mark her 200th birthday in 1997, and in 2012 to commemorate the 200th anniversary of her victory over HMS *Guerriere*.

Despite being a museum ship, *Constitution* remains a fully commissioned US Navy ship, with a crew of 60 officers and sailors, all active-duty US Navy personnel who participate in ceremonies, educational programmes and special events. The frigate is usually berthed at Pier 1 of the former Charlestown Navy Yard in Boston, USA, but her duties were interrupted in 2015 when she entered dry dock to begin a three-year restoration programme in the same yard.

USS *Constitution* sailed under her own power for
her 200th birthday in 1997, and once more in
August 2012, to commemorate the 200th
anniversary of her victory over HMS *Guerriere*.

# 36 : Boathook

## 1800

It is hard to imagine that the simple boathook was not developed during the Iron Age. It is, after all, only a metal hook attached to the end of a pikestaff (a spiked staff for use on slippery ground). Remarkably, the first recorded use of a boathook is in 1800, aboard the Meikle ferry that transported passengers across the Dornoch Firth in Scotland.

The metal hook is fashioned with a blunt tip for pushing away when undocking, and an inward curling hook to pull things out of the water, grapple mooring rings and pick up lines when docking.

Although many sailors still use a conventional boathook, whether it is constructed of wood or metal, there have been a number of recent innovations that have attempted to make the boathook work much harder. A device called the Hook & Moor pulls the mooring rope through the cleat or ring in a single motion, meaning that the ropes do not need to be thrown from a distance. Developments such as the Wrino boathook and the Dockingstick enable the mooring line to be held in a loop. Once the loop has been made on the boathook, the boathook and loop can be held over a cleat or piling without the sailor ever having to leave the boat.

The Royal Navy developed a ceremonial boathook drill when berthing and unberthing their ship's boats while officers and VIPs are aboard. Seamen are positioned fore and aft, waving their poles in unison. They would start with the poles in a vertical position, raise them horizontally above their heads, then lower them to shoulder height and finally to the hips before swinging the poles round to face the opposite direction.

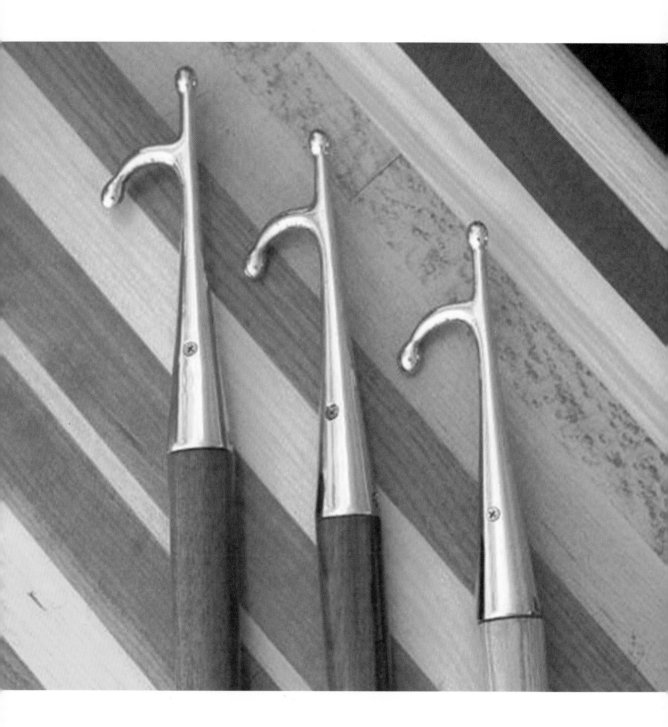

Although many modern boathooks are made of metal,
the traditional wooden boathook does the job just as
well and is an attractive accessory on a wooden boat.

# 37 : Portsmouth Block Mills

## 1802

During Nelson's lifetime, the Royal Navy got through more than 100,000 wooden sheave blocks – pulleys with a grooved wheel to hold a rope – a year. Each ship would use around 1,000 sheave blocks annually in various sizes. Up until that time, all were made by hand, which led to inconsistent quality and problematic supply.

To solve the problem, the brilliant engineer Isambard Kingdom Brunel was commissioned to create the first mass production line to produce standardised blocks. Built in Portsmouth Dockyard and powered by a stationary steam engine, the Block Mills opened in 1803 and by 1808 was producing 130,000 blocks a year.

Over a period of half a decade, Brunel arranged three series of machines into a production line, so that each stage of the work progressed to the next in a natural flow. The first set of machines to make medium blocks was installed in January 1803, the second set, for small blocks, in May 1803 and the third, for large blocks, in March 1805.

In total, the Block Mills housed 45 machines that included pin turning, circular saws and mortising machines, all driven by two 22.4kw steam engines. Such was the increase in the level of productivity that 10 men were now able to produce as many blocks as 110 skilled craftsmen.

The machines attracted a lot of attention from people like Admiral Lord Nelson, who made a tour of the mill on the morning he embarked for the Battle of Trafalgar in 1805, and Princess Victoria, who visited the facility as part of her education. The Block Mills have remained in Naval occupation ever since and though some machines were donated to the Science Museum in London and others are on display in Portsmouth's Dockyard Apprentice Museum, plans are afoot to preserve the mill and the remaining machinery.

Blocks like these were manufactured at the
Portsmouth Block Mills from the early 19th century
until the mid-1960s when production finally ended.

# 38 : Cloud names

## 1803

Before 1800, clouds had no names and were not well understood, with observers describing them simply as 'essences' floating in the sky. It was Englishman Luke Howard, a pharmacist and businessman, who gave these 'floating essences' their now familiar names when in 1803, he presented a paper to the Royal Meteorological Society in which he noted that there are three basic cloud shapes:

Heaps of separated cloud masses with cauliflower-shaped tops and flat bottoms, which he named *cumulus* (Latin for 'heap').

Layers of cloud much wider than they are thick, like a blanket or a mattress, which he named *stratus* (Latin for 'layer').

Wispy clouds, like a child's hair, which he called *cirrus* (Latin for 'curl').

To clouds generating precipitation, he gave the name *nimbus* (Latin for 'rain').

Howard's pioneering work also showed that clouds form in three layers within the lower atmosphere. Thus, with four types of clouds and three layers, he came up with 12 major cloud types.

Although he made his living as a businessman, heading a company that made pharmaceutical chemicals, Howard's passion was for meteorology and he made a number of important contributions to the subject beyond his classification of clouds, publishing several books and significant papers on the subject. These were *The Climate of London* (1818 and 1830), *Seven Lectures on Meteorology* (1837), *A Cycle of Eighteen Years in the Seasons of Britain* (1842) and *Barometrographia* (1847).

Sailors have for centuries used cloud shapes to forecast changing weather. For example, stable stratocumulus clouds are a sign that winds will be relatively light and conditions will remain unchanged for some hours. Conversely, rain-bearing cumulonimbus clouds will create areas of higher pressure that are filled with winds and can lead to potentially gusty conditions. Sea breezes are marked by distinct lines of cumulus clouds that form along the coasts as moist sea air is blown onto the coast. The classification of clouds allowed the definition of weather conditions to be standardised making communication of changes in the weather easier and more effective.

**HEAPS (CUMULUS FAMILY CLOUDS)** Fair weather cumulus |
Swelling cumulus | Cumulus congestus

**LAYERS (STRATUS FAMILY CLOUDS)** Stratus | Altostratus |
Cirrostratus

**LAYERED HEAP CLOUDS** Stratocumulus | Altocumulus |
Cirrocumulus

**PRECIPITATING RAIN CLOUDS** Cumulonimbus | Cirrus |
Nimbostratus

# 39 : Beaufort Scale

## 1805

Before Commander Francis Beaufort came up with his wind force scale in 1805, there was no way to annotate the strength of the wind. The cup anemometer used to measure the speed of the wind would not be invented for another four decades, so it was left to the imagination to describe conditions between a 'fair breeze' and 'blowing dogs off chains'.

Beaufort joined the Royal Navy at the age of 13 and rose to become a Rear Admiral and Knight Commander of the Bath. He invented his descriptive Beaufort scale in 1805 while commanding HMS *Woolwich*, a 44-gun man-of-war. It took a great deal of time to be recognised, and was not mandatory for log entries on all RN ships until 1838. Yet Beaufort's idea to associate a set of integers between 0 and 12 with descriptive sea states has stood the test of time.

At the heart of Beaufort's scale is the effect of the wind on his 18th-century fighting ship, the focus being on the ship and not the wind. Beaufort numbers 0 to 4 describe the wind in terms of the speed at which it would push the ship, those for 5 to 9 in terms of her sail carrying ability and those for 10 to 12 in terms of her survival. Beaufort's scale even made the jump from wind force to wind speed thanks to a maritime catastrophe.

In 1854, England and France were fighting in the Crimean War, in an alliance against Russia, their ships blockading the Black Sea port of Sevastopol. On the morning of 14 November, their combined fleet carrying almost all of their winter supplies was struck by an intense, early winter storm, and within 12 hours their losses exceeded those of any previous action at sea. The enquiries that followed led to the formation of a joint British/French weather network, the forerunner to the World Meteorological Organization, in order to forecast future storms.

By now Samuel Morse had developed the first practical telegraph and TR Robinson had invented the cup anemometer, so it was possible to transmit weather data around the world. The problem was that the world, particularly in areas inland, did not yet appreciate the effect that wind density had on speed readings. Thus, a man standing in the wetter areas of Central Europe might observe 37 revolutions of his anemometer, and record this as Beaufort force 7, but his colleague in the drier air of Missouri, USA, would count the same number of revolutions and send in his record as Beaufort force 5.

In 1912, the International Commission for Weather Telegraphy set about developing a universal set of velocity equivalents for the Beaufort scale, which was finally accepted in 1926 and revised slightly in 1946. In 1955, wind velocities in knots replaced Beaufort numbers on weather maps, but there was still a need for seamen to make visual estimates. Thus it became important to relate the seaman's guess logged in Beaufort numbers to the wind speed given in knots.

| NUMBER | WIND SPEED | | DESCRIPTION | WAVE HEIGHT | | SEA CONDITIONS | LAND CONDITIONS |
|---|---|---|---|---|---|---|---|
| | mph | kts | | m | ft | | |
| 1 | >1 | >1 | Calm | 0 | 0 | Flat | Calm. Smoke rises vertically. |
| 1 | 1–3 | 1–2 | Light air | 0.1 | 0.33 | Ripples without crests | Wind motion visible in smoke. |
| 2 | 3–7 | 3–6 | Light breeze | 0.2 | 0.66 | Small wavelets. Crests of glassy appearance, not breaking. | Wind felt on exposed skin. Leaves rustle. |
| 3 | 8–12 | 7–10 | Gentle breeze | 0.6 | 2 | Large wavelets. Crests begin to break; scattered white caps. | Leaves and smaller twigs in constant motion. |
| 4 | 13–17 | 11–15 | Moderate breeze | 1 | 3.3 | Small waves | Dust and loose paper raised. Small branches begin to move. |
| 5 | 18–24 | 16–20 | Fresh breeze | 2 | 6.6 | Moderate (1.2m) longer waves. Some foam and spray. | Branches of a moderate size move. Small trees begin to sway. |
| 6 | 25–30 | 21–26 | Strong breeze | 3 | 9 | Large waves with foam crests and some spray | Large branches in motion. Whistling heard in overhead wires. Umbrella use becomes difficult. Empty bins may tip over. |
| 7 | 31–38 | 27–33 | High wind, moderate, gale, near gale | 4 | 13.1 | Sea heaps up and foam begins to be blown in streaks in wind direction | Whole trees in motion. Effort needed to walk against the wind. Swaying of tall buildings may be felt especially by people on upper floors. |
| 8 | 39–46 | 34–40 | Fresh gale | 5.5 | 18 | Moderately high waves with breaking crests forming spindrift. Streaks of foam | Twigs broken from trees. Cars veer on road. |
| 9 | 47–54 | 41–47 | Strong gale | 7 | 23 | High waves (6–7m) with dense foam. Wave crests start to roll over. Considerable spray. | Larger branches break off trees, and some small trees blow over. Temporary signs and barricades blow over. Damage to large tents and canopies. |
| 10 | 55–63 | 48–55 | Whole gale, storm | 9 | 29.5 | Very high waves. Large patches of foam from wave crests give the sea a white appearance. Considerable tumbling of waves with heavy impact. Large amounts of airborne spray reduce visibility. | Trees are broken off or uprooted, saplings bent and deformed, poorly attached roof tiles in poor condition may peel off roofs. |
| 11 | 61–72 | 56–63 | Violent storm | 11.5 | 37.7 | Exceptionally high waves. Very large patches of foam, driven before the wind cover much of the sea surface. Very large amounts of airborne spray severely reduce visibility. | Widespread vegetation damage. More damage to most roofing surfaces, roof tiles may be blown away completely. |
| 12 | >73 | >63 | Hurricane force | >14 | >46 | Huge waves. Sea is completely white with foam and spray. Air is filled with driving spray. | Considerable and widespread damage to vegetation, a few windows broken. |

# 40 : Liquid compass

## 1813

We can thank the Chinese for the magnetic compass, with the first example dating back to the Han Dynasty in 206 BC.

The Chinese compass used a spoon-shaped lodestone (that automatically faces south) set on a flat, bronze plate marked with constellations and cardinal points. As the plate moved, the lodestone spun, coming to rest in a north–south orientation with the handle pointed south. An alternative style involved placing an iron needle that had been rubbed with a lodestone onto a piece of wood that was then floated in a bowl of water. The water allowed the wood to spin until the iron oxide needle was pointing south. However, it took another two millennia before the world had a fluid-damped practical pointer damped to limit swing and improve readability at sea.

Sir Edmund Halley introduced the first rudimentary working model of a liquid compass at a meeting of the Royal Society in 1690, but it was not until 1813 that Englishman Francis Crow patented a practical version. His design utilised a copper bowl filled with alcohol, with a float made from copper which had the points of the compass painted on top. A weight was used to keep the float in a horizontal position, while the float bore a magnetic needle. The bowl of liquid was covered with a sheet of thick glass and the compass was supported on two arms on a gimbal.

In 1860, US physicist and inventor Edward Samuel Ritchie patented a liquid marine compass that was superior in operation to Crow's although the patent was almost identical. The US Navy adopted the design shortly afterwards. Although there was limited use of liquid damped compasses on some Royal Navy ships and smaller boats from around 1830, the service continued to use the dry-mounted compass until 1908. It was at this point that the operational advantages of using the liquid compass in heavy seas and under heavy gunfire instead of dry-mounted designs, such as the Kelvin compass, became apparent.

A large liquid compass on a traditional wooden yacht. It is mounted on deck close to the steering wheel. On many yachts, a liquid compass is mounted within the steering wheel.

# 41 : Fresnel lens lighthouse

## 1823

The problems of enhancing and directing light power in lighthouses was not solved until the mid-1820s when the French physicist Augustin-Jean Fresnel installed the first example of what became known as the Fresnel lens in the Cordouan Light at Bordeaux, France.

The problem had tested scientists for centuries. The *Pharoes* are believed to have used beaten copper reflectors to increase the glow of their braziers. In 1777, William Hutchinson produced paraboloidal silvered mirrors that focused light in a narrow beam that increased light intensity by 400 times, but failed because the narrow beam could not be seen at all outside that arc. That problem was finally overcome four years later with the invention of the revolving beam concept which created the well-known flashing pattern. The first of these was installed in the Swedish lighthouse at Carlsten, Marstrand.

Fresnel made his breakthrough while working to reduce the weight of existing lenses. He discovered that the efficiency of a lens depends much more on the contours than on the thickness of the glass. By removing the excess glass from the outer prism shapes, he reduced the weight by a factor of ten, improved light capture to a level of 70 per cent and increased the reflectiveness from around 20,000 candlepower provided by the earlier Argand lamp mirror system to 80,000 candlepower – the equivalent to a modern car headlight. This was later improved to 100,000 candlepower when used with a pressurised oil lamp.

Fresnel then harnessed the refracting properties of glass by developing a series of concentric prisms that were moulded, then ground and polished individually to capture the light and reflect it outwards in a narrow horizontal beam. The vertical panels directly in front of the light were bull's-eye lenses surrounded by concentric prismatic rings. The panels directly above and below were curved prisms topped by a beehive-shaped lens to redirect the light at a more acute angle.

To refocus light that would otherwise be lost up into the sky or down towards the ground, Fresnel added angled mirrors at the top and bottom of the lens, together with a series of triangular prisms on the floor and ceiling to collect stray light and redirect it out through the lens. The additional advantage of this design was that the individual components, which together added up to many hundreds of pieces of glass, were much easier to transport than earlier mirrors and the individual prisms could be replaced easily.

Fresnel later developed a modified version of his lens system to produce a cylindrical drum lens that provided an all-round light. This eliminated the need for any form of rotating mechanism and are still in wide use today to project the flashing lights on buoys and beacons. His original rotating lens

At 14m high, the Makapuu Point Light on the
island of Oahu, Hawaii has the largest lens of
any lighthouse in the USA.

system weighed more than 11,000lb (5000kg) half
of which were the four glass lenses. The turntable
rotated in a cast-iron trough of mercury which
minimised friction. It was driven by a weighted
clockwork motor though later models, fitted with
acetylene gas lights, were turned using the same
pressurised gas. Fresnel's principles remain
valid today though the latest lenses are now
moulded in plastic, stand no taller than 2ft 6in
(76cm) and rely on electricity to power a 250w
lamp as well as the rotating platform which runs
on ball bearings.

# 42 : The first telegraph

## 1832

Samuel Morse, of Morse Code fame, was a famous portrait painter before getting involved in any kind of telegraph signalling. His change in profession came about due to the sudden death of his wife. At the time of the tragedy, he was fulfilling a commission to paint the Marquis of Lafayette in Washington, DC, when a horse messenger delivered a letter from his father stating, 'Your dear wife is convalescent'. This was followed the next day with an equally abrupt missive detailing his wife's passing. Morse packed up his paints and headed home immediately to New Haven, Connecticut, leaving the portrait of Lafayette unfinished. But by the time he arrived, his wife had already been buried. Heartbroken, he decided to explore a means of rapid long distance communication.

It was some years later during a voyage back from Europe that Morse had the good fortune to meet Charles Thomas Jackson, an expert in electromagnetism. After watching Jackson experiment with his electromagnet, Morse developed the concept of a single-wire telegraph, which he patented in 1832.

A year later, William Cooke and Professor Charles Wheatstone learned of the work that German inventors Wilhelm Weber and Carl Gauss were undertaking independently in order to develop an electromagnetic telegraph, and in 1836, they went on to build a small electrical telegraph within three weeks. Wheatstone discovered that a single large battery would not carry a telegraphic signal over long distances and concluded that numerous small batteries would be more successful.

Cooke and Wheatstone patented their electrical telegraph in May 1837, and within a short time had provided the Great Western Railway with a 13-mile (21km) stretch of telegraph. However, within just a few years, Cooke and Wheatstone's multiple-wire signalling method was overtaken by Morse's cheaper system ... and the rest is history.

A contemporary illustration showing the
simplicity of Samuel Finley Breese Morse's
(1791–1872) first single-wire telegraph apparatus.

# 43 : *Ann McKim* – first clipper ship

## 1833

Surprisingly perhaps, it did not occur to ship owners and designers to build ocean-crossing sailing ships that could sail at speed until the 1830s. Viking ships apart, most ships were brick shaped, in order to carry the largest load for a given time.

It was Isaac McKim, a leading entrepreneur from Baltimore, USA, who first thought of the idea to scale up the lines of the small Baltimore trading clippers to build a 494-ton 'ocean greyhound', in order to ply the China and South American trade routes. Measuring 143ft (43.5m) overall and 31ft (9.5m) beam, his new ship had a draft of 17ft (5.2m) aft and was named after McKim's wife, Ann. The new ship was renowned for the grace of her lines and was described in glowing terms by the author, Robert E Peabody: 'Her frame was of live oak and much mahogany and brass was used in decoration regardless of cost. She carried twelve brass cannon … Not only was she the best-known American ship afloat at the time, but she was also conceded to be the fastest, and her swift passages led others to copy her lines. Thus, she was the first of many clipper ships built during the next twenty-five years culminating in ships like the *Flying Cloud*.' Others have described her as an enlarged clipper schooner rigged as a ship.

Among her many accomplishments, the *Ann McKim* sailed from New York, USA, to Anjer (Anyer) in Indonesia in 79 days in 1842, and made the return voyage the following year in 96 days. However, her sailing life was cut sadly short. Like so many clipper ships, *Ann McKim* ended her days as a pontoon ship under the Chilean flag and was scrapped in 1852, just 19 years after she was first launched.

Within the image, caption text reads:

CLIPPER SHIP "ANN McKIM"

A colour print of the *Ann McKim* showing the
elegance of her lines. It was made in around 1920,
nearly 70 years after the ship was scrapped.

# 44 : Navigation lights

## 1836

It is chastening to think about how many ships were lost at sea prior to the first attempt to force captains to show lights at night. In 1836, a British Royal Commission made recommendations that every steamship should carry lanterns visible in all directions between sunset and sunrise, but it was another two decades before anyone took the issue seriously. By then 3,064 collisions involving British ships were recorded in one year, resulting in the loss of nine steamships and 270 sailing vessels.

It was a Captain Evans who finally solved the problem in 1849, by devising a forward-facing white masthead light for steamships within an arc two points abaft the beam on either side, along with the red and green sidelights on port and starboard sides, showing from right ahead to two points abaft the beam. Sailing vessels, however, would need only to carry a single white light until 1858, when both red and green sidelights were finally made mandatory for these vessels, too. The first International Maritime Conference in 1889 finally saw the USA and other nations fully recognise the importance of navigational lights on ships to prevent collisions.

Today, the International Maritime Organization determines the navigational lights to be carried aboard ships, and it has set detailed criteria based on the size and type of vessel. The purpose of the lights is to allow other vessels to determine both the length and the heading (or angle) of travel of the ship, so that in darkness they can avoid the vessel in its entirety, and take evasive action should the lights indicate. The standard system is red lights on the left of a ship (port side), green on the right (starboard) and white at the back (aft or stern) and front (fore/bow). The lights need to be fully visible head-on and '22.5 degrees abaft the beam'.

The introduction of effective navigation lights undoubtedly prevented many unnecessary collisions at sea, especially in channels with heavy shipping, leading to fewer sinkings and consequent loss of life.

There are standard placements for navigation lights on all vessels, from rowing boats, yachts and power boats, to fishing boats and tankers.

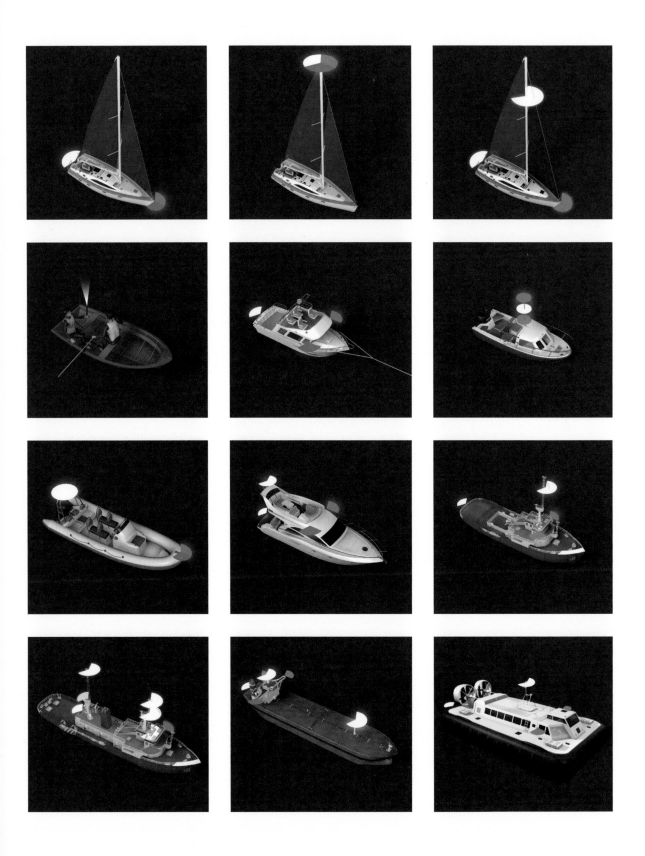

# 45 : Sou'wester

## 1837

The instantly recognisable waterproof sailor's hat known as the Sou'wester can be traced back to US fishermen from the port of Gloucester, Massachusetts, who developed the hat in order to keep themselves dry while fishing out on the Grand Banks. The name stems from the fact that bad weather across the Grand Banks invariably comes from the north-west, so you want to be facing towards the south-west to keep your face dry.

Originally, the Sou'wester was made from cotton sailcloth waterproofed with yellow linseed oil. The hat has a distinctive wide back brim that lies over the collar to prevent water from running down the wearer's neck, while the narrow brim at the front folds back to act as a gutter to drain away the water. The National Museum of American History holds a 19th century version known as the 'Cape Ann Sou'wester', which was used in the fisheries around Cape Ann in Massachusetts. It is made from oiled canvas and lined with flannel.

This sailor's friend has stood the test of time and there are plenty of foul weather clothing manufacturers who still have Sou'westers for sale in their catalogues. Modern versions are constructed from PVC-coated cotton and polyester, and many have additional features including fleece linings and ear flaps, to keep the wearer warm, and a stiff welded gutter in the top of the hat to stop water from running down the wearer's face. The Swedish firm Grundens has been making sou'westers and other waterproof garments since 1911. Their traditional yet high-tech sou'wester fared most admirably against similar products in a recent test and the firm is still renowned for the quality of their products, with many sailors hanging onto their Sou'westers for more than a quarter of a century.

Photographer Bert Hardy took this image of a trawlerman in his sou' wester and oilskins. It was originally published by *Picture Post* in a 1942 article called 'At Sea With Wartime Trawlermen'.

# 46 : *The Fighting Temeraire* by JMW Turner

## 1838

This iconic Turner painting is a quintessential depiction of a famous sailing ship and is at once magnificent, uplifting and tragic. Built at Chatham in 1898, the 98-gun HMS *Temeraire* was one of the last of the so-called second-rate ships and played a leading role in the British victory at the Battle of Trafalgar in 1805. She undertook a number of other missions in the defence of Britain, including the support of British operations along the Spanish coast and defending against Danish gunboat attacks in the Baltic with a final action off the French town of Toulon in 1813 during which she was fired on by shore batteries. She was then converted to a prison ship and moored on the River Tamar and later used as a receiving ship, as a guard depot and finally a guard ship. She remained in service until 1838 when she was decommissioned and towed from Sheerness to Rotherhithe in the Thames estuary to be broken up.

*Temeraire* appeared in a number of paintings including those depicting the Battle of Trafalgar, along with others of a fictionalised launch and her later service on the Medway. Turner's is the most renowned and the most poignant painting, depicting the famous ship being towed by paddlewheel steam tug on her last voyage to the breaker's yard. It was displayed at an exhibition at the Royal Academy in 1839.

The meaning of the painting has been debated at length. Many believe that it was intended to represent Britain's declining naval power. And although the ship is actually travelling in the wrong direction – east instead of west to Rotherhithe – and she was apparently pulled by two tugs rather than one, its purpose is not as an accurate record of the event but as a reflection of the sense of loss provoked by the breaking of the gallant ship. The marvellous sunset sets off the grace of the doomed *Temeraire*, with every mast and spar painted with accuracy, while the tug, by contrast, is small, dark and functional.

The painting was received with great acclaim. *The Morning Chronicle* of 7 May 1839 wrote that the painting represented 'the decay of a noble human being', while 'the gorgeous horizon poetically intimates that the sun of the *Temeraire* is setting in glory.' On 11 May, *The Literary Gazette* reflected that 'the sun of the glorious vessel ... setting in a flood of light ... [typified] the departing glories of the old *Temeraire*'. The painting remains beloved by many and was one of Turner's favourites as well. Although he lent it out once he could never bear to do so again and it was only on his death in 1851 that it was bequeathed to the nation and now hangs in the National Gallery in London.

The end of an era. Turner's painting of the last days
of *Temeraire* is both an elegy to and a celebration of
the days of the great sailing warships.

**46 :** *THE FIGHTING TEMERAIRE* **BY JMW TURNER, 1838**

# 47 : *Two Years Before the Mast* by RH Dana

## 1840

This is one of the best seagoing literature classics of all time. First published in 1840, the book recounts the hardships endured by the common seaman working his passage around Cape Horn from Boston, Massachusetts, to California and back.

Richard Henry Dana, Jr. was an undergraduate studying at Harvard University when he contracted measles, which affected his vision. Medical advice, it seems, recommended a sea voyage, though whether or not the doctor prescribed shooting the Horn during the southern winter in order to improve his sight goes unrecorded.

Dana left his studies to sign on as an ordinary sailor aboard the American brig *Pilgrim* in 1834 and returned two years later aboard the *Alert*. Keeping a detailed diary of his experiences, rather than using them to write an 'adventure of the sea', he set out to highlight how badly seamen were treated. In the end, he achieved both.

*Pilgrim* was a trading ship carrying goods from the East and bringing back cowhides picked up from Mexico, and San Diego, San Pedro Bay, Santa Barbara, Monterey Bay and San Francisco in the United States. Being well educated, Dana quickly picked up Spanish from the Californian Mexicans and became an interpreter on his ship. He also spent a season preparing hides for shipment back to Boston. His descriptions of the ports and accurate prediction of San Francisco's future growth and significance helped make the book a bestseller when the Gold Rush later attracted thousands to try their luck in the West, following in Dana's adventurous wake.

But it is his vivid descriptions of icebergs, horrendous seas and the need to race up and down ice-covered rigging to furl and unfurl sails that gets the reader's pulse racing and makes this book such an enduring classic. It was later made into a film, starring Alan Ladd, and released in 1946.

First published in 1840, *Two Years Before the Mast* has
been in print ever since and is still readily obtainable by
readers looking to discover a genuine maritime classic.

# 48 : Cup anemometer

## 1846

The Reverend John Thomas Romney Robinson was a man of many talents. A graduate from Trinity College, Dublin, he started his career as Deputy Professor of Physics at Trinity where he was also ordained as an Anglican priest. His prime interest was in astronomy and in 1823, aged 30, he became the resident astronomer at the Armagh Observatory where he remained until his death in 1882. It was here that he designed the modern cup anemometer.

This wind-speed measuring instrument had changed little in the intervening years since Leon Battista Alberti had invented the first mechanical anemometer in 1450. Others had made small improvements, but it was not until 1846 that TR Robinson made the instrument much more accurate by using four hemispherical cups each mounted on one end of four horizontal arms, which in turn were mounted at equal angles to each other on a vertical shaft. With the cups arranged symmetrically on the ends of the arms, the wind always has the hollow of one cup presented to it and is blowing on the back of the cup on the opposite side. By calculating the revolutions over a set time, this produces the average wind velocity for a wide range of speeds.

Robinson asserted that the cups revolved at one-third of the speed of the wind, whatever the cup size or arm length, but this in fact proved to be incorrect. It was later found that this anemometer factor depends on the dimensions of the cups and arms, and may have a value between two and three. Upon this discovery, every experiment involving an anemometer up to that point had to be repeated.

Later, in 1926, Canadian John Patterson developed a three-cup anemometer, which Brevoort and Joiner of the United States improved upon in 1935. In 1991, Derek Weston added the ability to detect wind direction and in 1994 Dr Andrews Pflitsch developed the sonic anemometer.

The four-cup pattern anemometer produced in 1846
remained in use for longer than most. This one was made
by the firm of F Darton and Company and is graduated in
miles and tenths of a mile to 500 miles. Smaller versions
are used today for hand-held instruments.

**48 : THE CUP ANEMOMETER, 1846**

# 49 : Signal flares

## 1848

So often in history we have made the mistake of underplaying the role wives have played in their husband's careers. But American inventor and businesswoman Martha Coston was one not to be underestimated, for she both perfected then patented the pyrotechnic flare.

When Coston's husband, a former naval scientist, died, he left behind a very rough sketch in a diary of plans he had for flares, which would allow for more effective communication between ships. The idea might have died with him had Martha not persevered to develop what was an elaborate system that she called 'Night Signals'. She initially developed red and white flares, adding a blue version after witnessing a firework display to celebrate the completion of the transatlantic telegraph cable.

In 1859, she registered the patent for flares and shortly thereafter the US Navy bought the patent rights for $5,000. The system went on to become the basis for the inter-ship communication that helped to save lives and win battles.

Martha Coston credited her late husband with the first patent, but in 1871, she received a patent for a design improvement that was exclusively her own. This was a system of flares based on colour and pattern, which made ship-to-ship and ship-to-shore communication possible. Martha Coston sold the US patent rights to the Navy for $20,000 and exported the idea to Denmark, France, Haiti, Holland and Italy. She died in 1904, an inventor in her own right and a very rich woman.

The system of signalling with flares used by modern sailors relies on the following conventions:

**White flares** are used to warn other ships of a boat's position in order to avoid collisions. They are also useful for illuminating the water at night if there is a man overboard.

**Orange distress flares** are designed to be used for distress calls in daylight as they are easier to see than red flares due to the substantial clouds of orange smoke that are produced.

**Red distress flares** are used only in an emergency that requires immediate assistance. Because of their meaning, it is illegal to fire or ignite a red flare either on the water or along the coast in order to prevent calling out emergency services for lesser reasons. Red distress flares are used mainly at night because they are easier to see in darkness.

A red flare is used where assistance is needed
urgently and allows the rescuers to determine
immediately the seriousness of the situation.

49 : SIGNAL FLARES, 1848

# 50 : Concrete boat

## 1848

The Romans pioneered the use of concrete as a construction material, and the roof dome on the Pantheon stands as a lasting tribute to this discovery. But who thought of using concrete to make boats, and did their first efforts lead to the coining of the phrase 'sink like a stone'?

The earliest ferro-cement boat is thought to be a dinghy built by the Frenchman Joseph-Louis Lamot in 1848 and exhibited at the Exposition Universelle in Paris seven years later. This simple double-ender is now displayed at the Museum at Brignoles, France.

Ferro-cement vessels are first shaped in steel mesh, which acts as the reinforcement and mould on top of which the concrete is trowelled. Ferro-concrete has relatively good strength and resistance to impact, and providing the steel reinforcement remains encapsulated and is not allowed to rust, it is also durable. The material is cheap and readily available, and in times of war has been used to build both barges and cargo vessels. The largest of these was the SS *Selma*, a 425ft (129m), 6800-ton (6,168-metric tonne) oil tanker launched in 1919, on the same day that Germany capitulated at the end of the First World War. A year later, she hit a jetty in Tamico, Mexico, ripping a 60ft (18m) hole in her hull, and though attempts were made to repair the damage, she was eventually scuttled along the Houston Ship Channel leading to Galveston, Texas, where she remains to this day.

Another concrete shipping relic from the First World War is the Nab Tower marking the eastern entrance to the Solent in the UK. During the war, 12 of these 10,000-ton (9000-metric tonne) concrete ship towers were planned to be floated out and sunk across the Varne Shoal in a line from Dungeness to Calais, in order to form an effective wall that would prevent German U-boats from entering the English Channel. Construction began in 1918 in Shoreham Harbour, where they became known as the 'Mystery Towers', for though 5,000 people were employed on their construction, very few knew for what task the towers were destined. By the time the war ended in 1918, only two towers had been completed, and after much discussion the first, the Nab Tower, was floated out to act as a navigation mark off Selsey Bill and her sister ship was demolished.

The 100ft (30.5m) steel cylindrical tower stands on an 180ft x 190ft (55m x 58m) concrete base created from a series of hexagonal shapes that rise like a cake in stepped stages. The concrete structure was designed to float and be scuppered once in position. The Nab Tower settled on the bottom at an angle and has the appearance of the nautical equivalent of the 'leaning tower of Pisa'. Yet the structure has survived countless storms and the impact from several ships running into it.

When the United States entered the Second World War in 1942, the US government contracted some

A concrete boat under construction. The outline is
made from a wire framework which adds literally a
'core of steel' before the concrete is poured on top of it.

6,000 workers to build 24 concrete supply ships in
Tampa, Florida, and even considered building a
submarine-shaped freighter, which her designer
claimed could achieve speeds of 75 knots. However,
the onslaught of war ended this research.

In more recent times, ferro-cement has become
popular among amateur boat builders, and a large
number of traditional long keel blue water cruising
yachts, like the Endurance range, have successfully
stood the test of time.

# 51 : America's Cup

## 1851

The America's Cup, yachting's premier trophy event, has always been something of a poisoned chalice, invariably bringing out the worst elements of sportsmanship. Originally known as the 'Auld Mug', the trophy was first contested in 1851, during which the American schooner *America* beat the cream of the British fleet in a 60-mile (96.5km) race around the Isle of Wight. *America*'s owners later renamed the trophy the America's Cup and donated it to the New York Yacht Club in order to encourage friendly match race competition between international yacht clubs. The first of these events was held in 1870 between James Lloyd Ashbury's topsail schooner *Cambria*, representing the Royal Thames Yacht Club, which was forced to race against not one but a 17-strong fleet of American defenders. *Cambria* finished a dismal eighth and Ashbury returned to the UK, convinced that the event had been anything but friendly.

It remained that way for the next 132 years, winning headlines like 'Britain Rules the Waves, but America Waives the Rules', until Australian Alan Bond, representing the Royal Perth Yacht Club, beat the Americans at their own game with the radical wing keeled 12m yacht *Australia 2* (see page 202). The Cup stayed in Australia for just one challenge, in 1987, when Dennis Conner's challenger, *Stars & Stripes*, representing the San Diego Yacht Club, whitewashed Iain Murray's *Kookaburra III 4:0*.

Conner and his San Diego syndicate leaders then dragged their feet in announcing the location of the next defence, suggesting either Hawaii (heavy weather) or San Diego (light airs) might be chosen. Potential challengers became impatient, unable to commence design work until a venue was announced. Many saw this as a deliberate ploy on the part of the defenders to give themselves a head start in design research. Banker Michael Fay, head of the New Zealand challenge, was so frustrated that he turned to the original deed of gift controlling the America's Cup and found that it should be challenger, rather than defender, driven. He issued an audacious challenge in a gigantic monohull named *New Zealand* with a 90ft (27m) waterline, the longest allowed under the original rules. The San Diego Yacht Club rejected what they called 'an unwelcome challenge' and continued to plan for match race series in 12m yachts.

However, Fay wasn't about to back down; he took the Californian club to the New York Supreme Court and won. The court ordered San Diego to either accept and negotiate mutually agreeable terms for a match, or to race under the default provisions of the deed, or forfeit the Cup to Fay's Mercury Bay Boating Club. Forced to race, Conner and his San Diego team chose to go for a spoiling defence, building a wing-masted catamaran that would easily outperform New Zealand's monohull challenge. Fay

The schooner *America* lines up against 17 other yachts
off Cowes for the race around the Isle of Wight that led
to the America's Cup. Five years later, *America*'s
owners presented the 100 Pound trophy to the New
York Yacht Club and renamed it the America's Cup.

cried 'foul', claiming that under the terms of the deed, the American's had to defend with a similar-sized monohull to the challenger. Once again, he turned to the New York Supreme Court for a ruling but was told to go race and complain afterwards. As expected, Conner's catamaran, *Stars & Stripes*, won at a canter, and Fay returned to the Court, only to lose on appeal.

The San Diego Yacht Club successfully defended the Cup again in 1992 in a new modern class of monohulls designed specifically for America's Cup match racing, but lost to a successful New Zealand challenge led by Sir Peter Blake and skippered by Russell Coutts in 1995.

The Cup went 'Down Under' for the next match in 2000, which Coutts and his crew won with ease against the Prada Challenge from Italy. But another upset occurred in the long history of the race, when Swiss biotech billionaire Ernesto Bertarelli moved to buy up the entire New Zealand A-team led by Coutts, who took up residence in Geneva to satisfy the loose nationality requirements of the Cup. Racing under the colours of the Société Nautique de Genève, the team returned to New Zealand in 2003 and won the trophy amid death threats from outraged Kiwis.

Coutts and his Alinghi crew of expats successfully defended the Cup in Valencia in 2007, but Bertarelli then sacked his able lieutenant Coutts, and fell foul of the America's Cup community by attempting to take control of both the defence and challenge trials. He was thwarted by software billionaire Larry Ellison, the second richest man in the United States, who brought Coutts in to mastermind his campaign and forced a match in 90ft waterline length multihulls with backing from the New York Supreme Court in 2010. Ellison's *Oracle BMW* won with ease.

The next match was in San Francisco Bay in 72ft wing-sailed foil-borne catamarans, amid accusations of cheating, spying and illegal use of design software once the Cup races had begun between Team New Zealand and Ellison's *Oracle*. To start with, the Kiwis were vastly superior both in speed and boat handling and won the first six races, only to see *Oracle* come from behind to win eight races in a row and the 19-race series on the final day. The next America's Cup will be staged in Bermuda in 2017 in smaller foiling catamarans.

*Oracle Team USA* skippered by James Spithill of Australia and *Emirates Team New Zealand* skippered by Dean Barker of New Zealand sailed in AC 72s carbon catamarans during race 7 on day four of the America's Cup on 14 September 2013 in San Francisco.

# 52 : Signal flags –
# International Code of Signals

## 1857

Whatever did sailors do to communicate before the advent of the International Code of Signals? Well, if a crew were in distress, it would fly its ensign upside-down. If pirates were about to attack, they might unfurl a Jolly Roger flag to warn their unsuspecting prey – but not until the last possible moment! From a very early age, ships did have code flags, but these signals invariably had regional interpretations and were not universally understood until 1857, when the British Board of Trade came up with the first commercial code.

This arrived in two sections: the first containing universal international signals, the second, British signals only. Eighteen separate signal flags were used to make over 70,000 messages. Vowels and some little-used letters were omitted to keep things simple and prevent the need to spell out any word that might be objectionable in another language.

During the First World War, the code was severely tested and found wanting. Too many signals were misread, including one where two warships turned in on each other instead of away, and collided. In 1932, a new code was adopted that worked in seven languages: English, French, German, Italian, Spanish, Japanese, and Norwegian. It also introduced vocabulary for aviation and a medical section.

This remained in use until 1964 when the newly formed Intergovernmental Maritime Consultative Organization (IMCO) launched the current international code, which shifted the focus from general communications to safety and also included Russian and Greek languages for the first time. This established a standardised alphabet made up of the letters A to Z and 10 digits and associated this alphabet with standardised flags.

The beauty of this system is that it matters not whether the senders and receivers speak different languages, for each has a book with the equivalent standardised messages keyed to the same code. For example, the master of a ship wishing to communicate with another ship when his radio is not working, or the call sign of the other ship is unknown, simply has to raise the Kilo flag or flash the 'dash-dot-dash' in Morse Code to be understood.

The alphabet and numeral flags of the International Code of Signals. Though they are rarely used to spell out words, they are invaluable for coded messages.

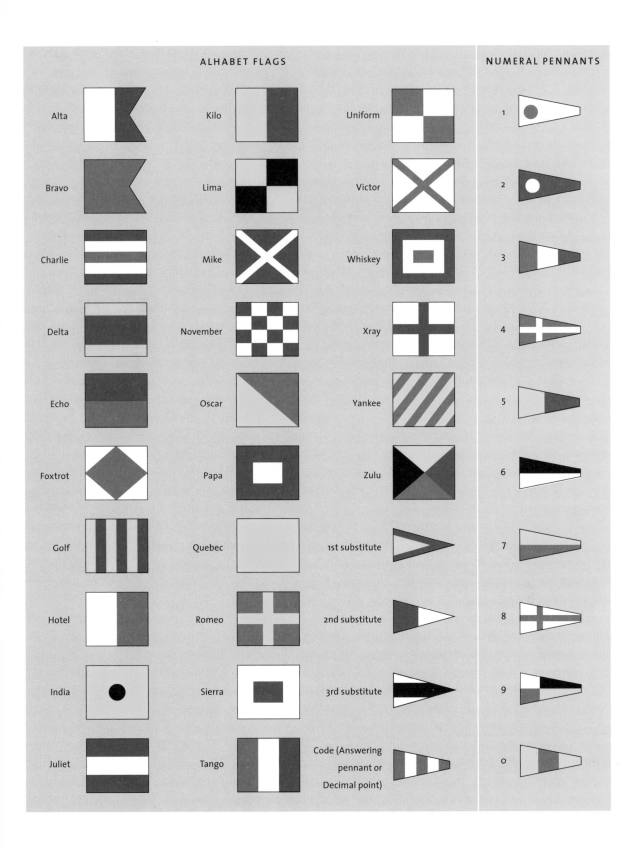

ALHABET FLAGS

NUMERAL PENNANTS

Alta

Bravo

Charlie

Delta

Echo

Foxtrot

Golf

Hotel

India

Juliet

Kilo

Lima

Mike

November

Oscar

Papa

Quebec

Romeo

Sierra

Tango

Uniform

Victor

Whiskey

Xray

Yankee

Zulu

1st substitute

2nd substitute

3rd substitute

Code (Answering
pennant or
Decimal point)

1

2

3

4

5

6

7

8

9

0

# 53 : Spinnaker

## 1865

Who invented the spinnaker, that colourful downwind parachute-shaped sail that can lead to equal amounts of delight and dread on board yachts? The date is right, but whether it was the Cowes-based yacht *Sphinx* that first set a spinnaker in the Solent or William Gordon's yacht *Niobe* remains open to debate.

The origins of the name are equally disputed and have been lost to time. It may have derived from 'Sphinx's Acre', which led eventually to spinnaker, or possibly a comment from one of *Niobe*'s crew: 'Now there's a sail to make her spin', becoming 'spin maker'. William Gordon was also known as 'Spinnaker Gordon'. And just to add spice to the mix, in the logbook of the USS *Constitution* for 13 July 1812 is the comment: 'From 12 to 4 AM moderate breezes and thick cloudy weather with rain at 1 AM hauled up the mainsail and set the spinnaker at half past 3 AM set the mainsail.' Did naval frigates really carry such sails?

Whatever its origins, it is very likely that the first spinnakers were symmetrical, so that they could be flown on either side from a spinnaker pole attached to the mast. The asymmetric spinnaker, or gennaker, did not appear until the 1980s when the owners of 18ft skiffs (the fastest class of sailing skiff) began to develop the concept of racing with large downwind jibs set from a long extending bowsprit. This then led to the asymmetric cruising chute, designed to simplify their setting without any poles on boats that are sailed short or singlehanded.

Paul Cayard's yacht *EF Language* won the 1997/8 Whitbread Round the World Race using the Code O asymmetric and its derivatives as a secret weapon. This light wind reaching sail, which could be roller furled like a genoa around its wire luff, is made from spinnaker cloth and was shaped to sail 10 degrees higher into the wind than any previous asymmetric. *EF Language* was the only yacht to carry this type of sail on the first leg of the race, where it proved perfect for sailing through the south-east trades and led to the vessel finishing first in Cape Town by an astounding 19-hour margin.

Yachts making use of symmetrical spinnakers when running with the wind. When correctly set, the leading edges of the spinnaker should be almost parallel to the wind.

52 · SPINNAKER, 1865

# 54 : *Cutty Sark*, last of the great clippers

## 1869

*Cutty Sark*, the sailing ship that has pride of place at Greenwich, South London, has a colourful history. Built in 1869 for the Jock Willis Shipping Line, *Cutty Sark* was one of the last tea clippers and coming at the end of a long period of design development, one of the fastest. But the rise in steam propulsion, coupled with the opening of the Suez Canal the same year as her launch, made all sailing tea clipper ships redundant within a few years.

This led *Cutty Sark*'s owners to turn their focus to the wool trade and for 10 years she ruled the seas between England and Australia. Part of her success is attributed to her Captain, Richard Woodget, who took command in 1885. A fearless navigator and successful man-manager, he got the best out of both ship and crew, taking them deep into the Roaring Forties to shorten the distance and gain most from gales that circulate around these latitudes. On his first voyage in command, *Cutty Sark* sailed from England to Sydney in 77 days, and returned to the UK in 73 days to establish herself as the fastest vessel to make the January wool sales in England.

When steam eclipsed sail, *Cutty Sark* was sold in 1895 to a Portuguese shipping company and renamed *Ferreira*. She continued as a cargo ship until bought by Wilfred Dowman, a retired sea captain, in 1922, who converted her into a training ship operating from Falmouth. After his death in 1938, *Cutty Sark* was transferred to the Thames Nautical Training College, Greenhithe, until 1954 when she was put on public display in a dry dock at Greenwich. Since then, the ship has twice been damaged by fire, first on 21 May 2007 while undergoing conservation, which led to a full restoration of the ship, and again on 19 October 2014, during which she suffered minor damage.

The ship's current display allows visitors to walk beneath her burnished keel, while retaining the view of masts and spars that has been a fixture of the Greenwich skyline for the past 60 years.

This painting by Brazendale Cunnelly of *Cutty Sark* sailing off the coast of China, alongside a Chinese junk, reflects her early years as a tea clipper, although she spent much of her career transporting wool from Australia.

# 55 : Walker speed log

## 1876

Sailors have been trying to compute speed since time was first invented. Back in the 16th century, the best method for calculating speed was to time how long a piece of wood dropped in the water from the bow would take to draw level with the stern. In 1578, Humfray Cole published his invention to log a ship's speed. This used a small boat fitted with a wheel and an axle-tree, which turned clockwise within the boat. It also had dials and pointers indicating fathoms, leagues, scores of leagues and hundreds of leagues.

In 1668, a Dr R Hooke was recorded to have shown a vane to members of the Royal Society that rotated as the vessel progressed, to indicate speed, and five decades later Sir Isaac Newton gave a disparaging report on the 'marine surveyor', a rotating log that Henry de Saumarez had developed. Others followed with improvements, until RH Gower demonstrated the registration of a vessel's speed through mechanical means in 1772.

Viscount de Vaux was first to develop a speed log using water pressure in 1807, and CE Kelway invented an electrical log in 1876, but it was Thomas Walker's harpoon or frictionless log, called the Ai Harpoon ship log, that showed the greatest promise. Two years later, Walker introduced the Cherub, the first model to provide an indicator on the ship's taff rail showing distance run under varying speeds.

Modern versions of the Walker speed log are set in a separate housing attached to the yacht's rail so that the speed can be simply monitored without the need to keep hauling the log in for reading.

# 56 : Fin keel

## 1880

The keel is essentially a flat blade that projects down into the water from the bottom of a sailing boat. It prevents 'leeway' (the wind blowing the boat sideways), and it contains the ballast that keeps the boat upright. On many traditional boats the keel is built into the hull, with the ballast either bolted to the bottom of the keel or set inside it. It makes for a sturdy, reliable design, but not for speed and manoeuvrability, so most modern yachts have 'fin' keels. These are usually cast in lead and bolted to the flattish bottom of the hull. Some fibreglass yachts have a moulded stub on the bottom to which the ballast is bolted. Fin keels are far more efficient than built-down keels at preventing leeway: the keel is drawn towards the windward side and tries to pull itself, and the boat, into the wind, thereby negating almost all of the wind-induced leeway, leaving just enough to continue to create lift around the keel.

The first recorded yacht to sport a fin keel was designed by Englishman EH Bentall in 1880. Named *Evolution*, she was anything but, and her failure to perform to windward was blamed on her low ballast ratio and narrow hull form. The US engineer and yacht designer Nathanael Herreshoff did somewhat better in 1991 with his 30ft *Dilemma*. The yacht had a cutaway forefoot and highly raked rudder post, and was the victor in every race it ever entered.

But no designer really mastered the science of fin keels until 1966, when Olin Stephens modified the underbody of Pat Haggerty's Sparkman & Stephens yacht *Bay Bea*, from its original long keel with rudder attached to a shorter keel and separate rudder. Stephens then perfected the concept in the test tank, leading to *Intrepid*, the first 12m yacht with a separate keel and rudder, which successfully defended the America's Cup in 1967 and 1970 after further modifications had been made to the hull.

A modern yacht standing in dry dock for refurbishing clearly shows the shape of its fin keel.

56 : FIN KEEL, 1880

# 57 : Sea anchor

## 1887

The sea anchor has been around since the invention of the bucket. Early models were often improvised from any spare parts that could be found aboard a ship, including sails to stabilise the position of even large vessels in heavy weather.

An 1877 US Naval Academy instruction book describes several methods of making a sea anchor using wooden or metal framework to support a simple, kite-like shape of canvas, backed with a net or closely spaced rope in order to provide strength.

A small anchor attached to one corner kept the sea anchor from twisting. If the framework was wooden, its buoyancy kept the sea anchor just beneath the water's surface, but the iron framework required a buoy to keep it at the proper depth. Today, the sea anchor has several names: drift anchor, drift sock, para-anchor and boat brake, and has become quite complex in design. There are models available for the pocket cruising yacht up to naval vessels and ocean-going tugs.

Their object is to prevent the vessel from lying side-on to the prevailing winds and facing the mercy of breaking waves. As such, the sea anchor is attached to a bridle running from bow to stern, in order for the vessel to be held at any desired angle to the wind and waves. The beauty of these sea anchors is the fact that they 'spill' water when under severe load, absorbing much of the shock loading on the anchor line each time the vessel is hit by a wave.

This important piece of kit can also be used to limit drift, or attached to a towed vessel to maintain tension on the towing line.

Resembling a mini parachute, the sea anchor holds
the bow pointing into the waves and lessens leeway.

# 58 : Colin Archer rescue boat

## 1892

olin Archer (1832–1921) was a Norwegian naval architect and boatbuilder born to Scottish parents who emigrated to Larvik in Norway before his birth, giving him Norwegian nationality but an English name.

He is best known for his distinctive double-ended sail boat designs, including *Fram*, used by Fridtjof Nansen and Roald Amundsen's Polar expeditions in 1893–1896 and 1910–1912 respectively. These boats proved so seaworthy that Archer was called upon to develop a lifeboat design for the Redningsselskapet (the Norwegian Society for Sea Rescue), which went into service in 1893 and saved 37 lives during a storm off the coast of Finnmark.

This prototype, *Colin Archer RS 1*, is now a floating museum in Oslo, Norway. Several other Redningsselskapet lifeboats are still sailing, including the *Frithjof Wiese RS40*.

In 1904, Archer built a boat named *Asgard* for the Irish writer Robert Erskine Childers, author of the novel *Riddle of the Sands*. A fierce nationalist, he used *Asgard* to smuggle guns during the Irish Civil War, before being caught and executed in 1922.

In 1928, William Atkin scaled down Archer's 47ft (14m) pilot rescue boat *Regis Voyager* to make the 32ft (9.8m) *Eric*. Both the Argentine sailor Vito Dumas and British sailor Robin Knox-Johnston used the *Eric* as a model for the yachts they constructed to complete their solo circumnavigations. Dumas set out from Buenos Aires in June 1942 in his ketch *LEHG II*, making just three landfalls on his travels round the fearsome Southern Ocean. Knox-Johnston's ketch-rigged *Suhaili* was a replica of the *Eric* design, and aboard *Suhaili*, he became the first man to circumnavigate the globe non-stop and singlehanded in 1969.

The *Stavanger* was built by Colin Archer in 1901 and served as a lifeboat for 37 years. In 2009 she made one last voyage along the Norwegian coast, from the Lofoten Islands in the north to Lindesnes in the south, followed by a passage up the Oslo fjord to the capital and the Maritime Museum, where she now resides.

# 59 : Binoculars

## 1893

Binoculars consist of two identical telescopes mounted side-by-side, which allow the viewer to use both eyes to gain a three-dimensional view at a distance. This is because the two optics are set at slightly different angles, and the merged view gives a sense of perspective when looking through it. Before the advent of binoculars, sailors would have had to use a telescope to see distant ships, locate land and view other objects. The development of binoculars allowed for a more controlled and focused viewing.

The original versions were known as Galilean binoculars, and matched convex lenses to concave eyepiece lenses, which gave them a very narrow field of view. Such a construction formed the basic design of opera glasses and other early 19th-century optics. But it was another 200 years before Johann Voigtländer, from Vienna, Austria, made further improvements by adding eye tubes to the binoculars, in order to provide focusing elements.

Perhaps the first true binocular revolution was the invention of porro-prism binoculars in 1854. Italian optician Ignazio Porro patented the first prism binoculars in 1854, with his system of twice-reflecting an image in internal mirrors so that it retained its natural orientation to the eye. The system wasn't commercially developed until 1894, when Carl Zeiss began selling the first recognisably modern binocular.

The design was later refined, first by Achille Victor Emile Daubresse and then by Moritz Carl Hensoldt, who developed the roof prism in 1897, which increased both the distance between the objective lenses and the depth of field, improving image quality considerably.

Porro-prism binoculars are generally small, and have a bright and true image. The design stayed popular through to the late 20th century, but roof-prism models gradually usurped the porro-prism's market-dominance. Roof prisms first emerged in the 1870s and were commercially patented in 1905, again by Carl Zeiss. The direct alignment of lenses in a roof prism meant that the barrels could be slimmer and more compact, but would lose a little comparative brightness.

The use of binoculars in sailing, particularly that of roof-prism models, has resulted in many technical innovations during the binoculars' evolution. Anyone who has ever tried to focus on a distant boat in drizzle or heavy rain will appreciate the development of waterproofing (via hermetic sealing to prevent water ingress) and fog proofing (through gas filling), both of which date from the early 1970s. A waterproof binocular has O-rings at each opening in its structure, which help with focusing and act as internal washers, while the entire space inside is injected with gas and completely sealed. The gas – most usually nitrogen – chemically prevents the

Although modern binoculars have benefited greatly from
new materials and better optics, in form and technology,
they remain very similar to the earliest models.

condensation caused by extreme changes and juxtapositions of temperature, while the absence of oxygen cuts down corrosion on the optics' internal workings. However, it is still not possible to prevent all of the actions of water vapour in optics, and even with the most expensive brands, users will find that the smallest amount of heat and/or water from their eyes may fog up their lenses in cold weather. Therefore, external rubber armour typically completes the sealing of a set of binoculars, preventing internal water damage as well as

protecting the outer casing. Most sets are also tested under water to check whether both the rubber armour and metal housing can withstand pressure of up to 16ft (5m) for five minutes.

The market for binoculars is packed with budget, mid-price and high-end options. Innovation remains ongoing, providing ever clearer, truer and brighter images. The development of the whole industry means that even entry-level binoculars can often be of a quality that only the best and most expensive could provide just a few short decades ago.

# 60 : *Yachting World*, oldest continuously published sailing magazine

## 1893

It was not the first publication of its kind, because the introduction within the pages of the first issue of *Yachting World* magazine alludes to rival rags. But *Yachting World*, first published in 1893, is undoubtedly the oldest continuously published sailing magazine.

The title began as a weekly newspaper devoted to covering the sport of sailing around the UK, with 'special correspondents' filing detailed reports from their own regions. The first editors remained anonymous, and so did the 'correspondents', because most had influential positions within the sport. The only author to be credited in the first edition was Herbert Russell who's 'Yachting Yarns' became a regular column. The first editor is believed to have been Major Brooke Heckstall-Smith, then secretary of the newly formed Yacht Racing Association, better known now as the Royal Yachting Association. His brother, Malden, became the second editor of *Yachting Monthly* magazine in 1921.

Some things in publishing never change, like 'Letters to the Editor', which was almost certainly written by the editor in that first *Yachting World* edition. It also carried a fulsome four-page profile on the Prince of Wales, clearly setting its sights high.

The magazine's first readers often had their copies bound into annual volumes, which can still be found in second-hand bookshops today. In May 1993, the current publishers printed a Centenary issue, which is now a collectors' item.

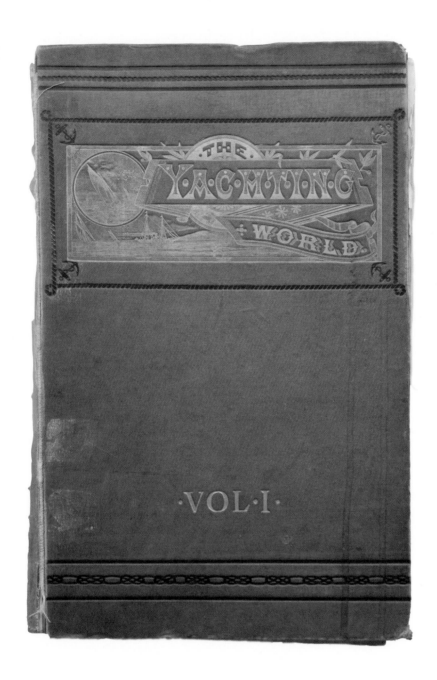

Packed with closely set type, the first edition of *Yachting World* was a far cry from the glossy, highly illustrated magazine of today – but its audience is probably very similar.

# 61 : *Sailing Alone Around the World* by Joshua Slocum

## 1900

Nova Scotian-born Joshua Slocum was the first man to circumnavigate the globe singlehandedly. He set sail from Boston, Massachusetts, on 24 April 1895, in the 36ft 9in (11.2m) Chesapeake Bay oysterman *Spray* and returned to Newport, Rhode Island, on 27 June 1898.

This remarkable feat went almost unnoticed. Instead, the Spanish–American War, which had begun two months earlier, dominated the headlines, and it was only after hostilities had come to a close that US newspapers began publishing articles describing Slocum's amazing adventure. These encouraged Slocum to write a book of his own in 1900, titled *Sailing Alone Around the World*, an enduring classic that remains in print to this day.

Slocum had run away to sea aboard a Nova Scotian fishing boat at the age of 16 and graduated to chief mate aboard a series of British ships. He settled in San Francisco in 1865 and became a US citizen. After a period of salmon fishing and fur trading, he returned to the sea to pilot a trading schooner between San Francisco and Seattle. His first command was the barque *Washington*, which he sailed from San Francisco across the Pacific, to Australia, and back home via Alaska in 1869.

Slocum continued trading across the Pacific for the next 13 years before washing up in Fairhaven,

Massachusetts, where he was offered *Spray* free of charge. He set about restoring her, intending to circumnavigate the globe.

His dream finally began in the spring of 1895, and took him first to his boyhood home at Brier Island, Nova Scotia, before he set out across the Atlantic to Gibraltar via the Azores then across to the South American ports of Pernambuco, Rio de Janeiro, Montevideo and Buenos Aires, before cutting through the Magellan Straits to the Pacific.

Slocum navigated without a chronometer, relying instead on dead reckoning for longitude, which required only a cheap tin clock for approximate time, and noon-Sun sights for latitude. With her long keel and balanced rig, *Spray* was capable of keeping a course relative to the wind and Slocum sailed 2,000 miles (3,219km) west across the Pacific without once touching the helm. He stopped at the Cocos Islands and Mauritius before rounding the Cape of Good Hope in Christmas 1897, then re-crossed the Atlantic via St Helena and Ascension Island to the Caribbean, reaching Newport, Rhode Island, in summer 1898.

Slocum had signed with a publisher before setting out on his circumnavigation and sent him several letters en route. *Sailing Alone Around the World* garnered great reviews, not least from fellow author Arthur Ransome, who wrote: 'Boys who do not like

Joshua Slocum, pictured on his yacht *Spray*. Although he
tried to settle on dry land following his great solo
voyage, the pull of the sea was too strong, and Slocum,
who could not swim, was lost at sea on his final voyage.

this book ought to be drowned at once'; Slocum's
story was serialised in *The Century* magazine and
has been reprinted many times since.

By 1909, however, Slocum's funds were running
low and he began planning for a new adventure
aboard *Spray*, exploring the Orinoco, Rio Negro and
Amazon Rivers with the hope of another book deal. On
14 November 1909, he set sail for the West Indies on
one of his usual winter voyages and was never heard
from again. In July 1910, his wife informed the
newspapers that she believed Slocum to have been lost
at sea. He was declared legally dead in 1924.

# 62 : Sheet winch

## 1903

How many winches do you have on your boat? The answer is likely to be none, for the common sheet and halyard winch is, in fact, a capstan. By definition, a winch stores its cable on the drum and is mounted horizontally. By contrast, 18th-century sailors had to work together to push the ship's enormous capstan windless when weighing anchor. But that massive device is the forerunner to what we call the sheet winch today.

Before the use of winches to control sails, even the largest ships were reliant on a simple block and tackle device. This limited the size of sails and led to the need for multiple small sails, especially on larger ships. Since then, small snubbing winches have been in use on yachts since the late 19th century. The first versions were geared 1:1 and turned clockwise on a ratchet. The snubbing winch rotates as the rope is pulled and gains rope from the loaded end of the winch. Easing the tension allows the turns to slip on the drum so that the rope is paid out. It can be stopped (snubbed) by restoring the tension at the tail. A handle fitted at the centre of the winch allows greater force to be applied.

It was Nathanael Herreshoff, the design guru behind so many successful America's Cup defenders, who first introduced the large deck winch in order to control large sheets aboard his yacht *Reliance* in 1903. These winches were so hard-wearing that they were handed down first to *Resolute* in 1920 and then to *Enterprise* in 1930.

Sheet winches did not become commonplace on smaller yachts until after the Second World War. British yachtsmen Len Lewery and Leslie Marsh invented the modern top-action winch in 1953, manufacturing them under the Lewmar brand. Six years later, they were joined by Henry Shepherd (whose company made helicopter gearboxes for Westland), and he used his knowledge of lightweight aeronautical materials to develop the multispeed winch we recognise today.

A modern sheet winch is a highly effective way of
managing a yacht's sheets without a huge amount
of physical effort from the person sailing her.

# 63 : Radar

## 1904

Radio waves were first discovered in the late 19th century when the German scientist Heinrich Hertz showed that metallic objects reflected the waves. However, it was not until the early 20th century that we began to harness the principles of electromagnetism. It was another German inventor, Christian Hülsmeyer, who first used radio waves in order to build a simple ship detection device intended to help prevent collisions in fog.

Hülsmeyer's Telemobiloscope had a mechanism to synchronise the aiming direction of the receiving antenna with a compass-like indicator, and could also differentiate false signals. However, it could not indicate range with any degree of accuracy, and confidence in the system eroded.

Other systems were developed over the next two decades, but it was during the build-up to the Second World War that progress was really made when it was determined that the timing of pulses read on an oscilloscope gave an accurate account of range.

Britain, France, Germany, Holland, Italy, the United States and Russia all worked in great secrecy to develop radar systems, but it was the United States Army Signals Corp that coined the term RADAR. During the war, Britain took a lead in these developments with the invention of the magnetron, which it shared with the United States and four Commonwealth countries: Australia, Canada, New Zealand and South Africa. This advance in communication was one of the deciding factors in determining the outcome of the war.

Modern applications of radar for sailors include marine radar, which measures the bearing and distance of ships in order to prevent collisions at sea, and allows them to navigate and fix their position at sea when in range of shore or other reference points including buoys, lighthouses and islands. When ships are in port or harbour, radar systems that manage traffic are used to monitor and control the movements of craft in busy waters.

Radar proved invaluable in war at sea. Here a US Navy technician marks radar data on a chart, tracking enemy Japanese ships in the Pacific Theatre during the Second World War.

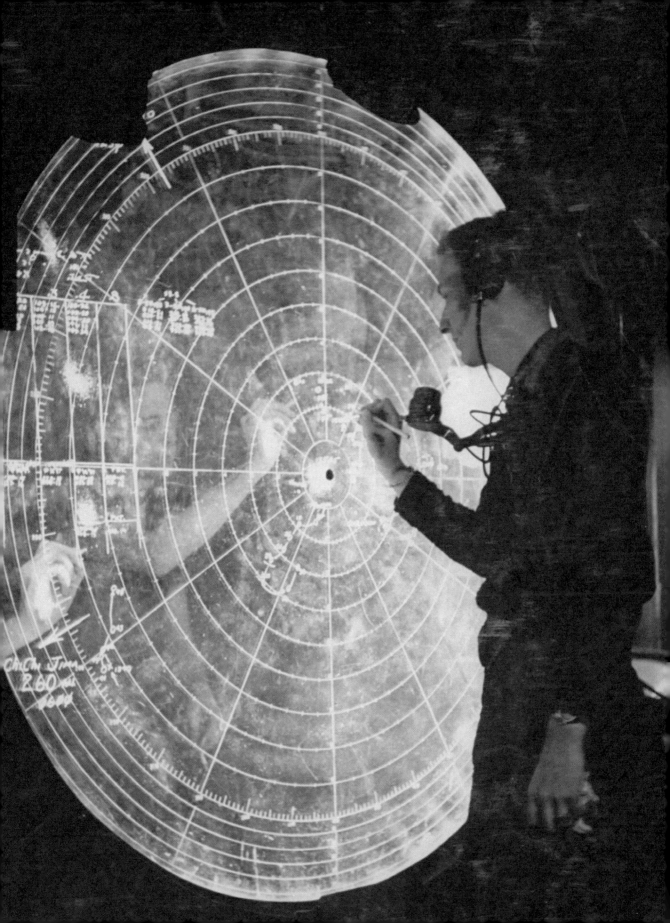

# 64 : Wykeham Martin roller furling gear

## 1907

Sailors frequently have to furl their sails at short notice, to combat sudden squalls and when laying anchor at night. It was Major Ed du Boulay who first came up with the idea of a furling jib (a method of furling the sail), at the turn of the 20th century. The basic design operated like a roller blind, with a swivel inside the lower drum that took the furling line. However, the luff of the sail rolled round a pine pole, which caused wear on the forestay and also discoloured the sail.

Cue fellow Englishman Colonel Wykeham-Martin, who realised that the jib would furl around its own luff rope without the need for a wooden luff tube. He also incorporated roller bearings into the lower drum and patented the system in 1907. It is still made today, cast in solid bronze.

The jib is attached to swivels at tack and head of the sail, the lower one having a furling line wound around the spool. When the line is pulled, the furler turns, rolling up the jib; when the furling line is released, the jib sheet is pulled on to unfurl the sail. The system does have its limitations, for, as it is not attached to the forestay, it is difficult to control the luff tension on all craft except dinghies and pocket cruising yachts.

Murray Scheiner, a rig designer from Great Neck, New York, addressed the issue when he modernised the jib furling system for larger yachts in the late 1960s. His inspiration came from watching a disabled sailing friend who required several crewmembers to hoist the jib, which prevented him from sailing independently. Scheiner's solution was to encase the forestay in a luff foil to which the headsail was attached. This resolved the problem of luff sag, and a larger drum and top swivel made it easier to furl and unfurl the sail.

Opposite, above: A modern roller furling system.
Right: A traditional brass Wykeham Martin
roller furling system.

64 : WYKEHAM MARTIN ROLLER FURLING GEAR, 1907

# 65 : *Bluenose*, historic schooner

## 1921

There are few more iconic symbols in Nova Scotia's history than the 160ft 9in (49m) fishing schooner *Bluenose*. Launched in 1921, she became a symbol of everything good about the region during the 1930s, and appeared on everything, from postage stamps to coins. Even today, she is still depicted on vehicle number plates.

The celebrated racing ship and fishing vessel was built to avenge the defeat of the Nova Scotian fishing schooner *Delawana* by the Gloucester, Massachusetts fishing schooner *Esperanto* in a race sponsored by the Halifax Herald newspaper in 1920. The name 'Bluenose' is an 18th-century nickname for Nova Scotians and an apt name for this rugged vessel. After spending the 1930 fishing season working the Grand Banks of Newfoundland under the command of Angus Walters, *Bluenose* defeated the Gloucester vessel *Elsie* to return the International Fishermen's Trophy to Nova Scotia. She

was later defeated 2-0 in the inaugural Sir Thomas Lipton International Fishing Challenge Cup by perhaps her most celebrated competitor, the *Gertrude L. Thebaud*, but over the next seven years, no challenger – American or Canadian – could take the title from her.

Fishing schooners became obsolete during the latter part of the 1930s, overtaken by motor trawlers, but despite efforts to keep *Bluenose* in Nova Scotia, she was sold to work in the West Indies. Laden with bananas, she struck a coral reef off Île-à-Vache, Haiti, in 1946. Wrecked beyond repair, she was abandoned on the reef and though divers and filmmakers claim to have located the wreck, as recently as 2005, the large number of wrecks on the reef has made it difficult to confirm identification.

The vessel was later commemorated through the replica schooner *Bluenose II*, which was launched in 1963 and since restored and relaunched in 2013.

*Bluenose II*, a replica of her legendary namesake is
seen sailing off the coast of Nova Scotia.

# 66 : *Avenger*, first planing dinghy

## 1928

The year 1928 was a vintage one for dinghy racing, and one during which great advances were made in construction, design and rigs. The most significant advance in the Northern Hemisphere was *Avenger*, an International 14-class dinghy, designed and built by the English sailing innovator Uffa Fox. She proved far ahead of her time, winning 52 of her 57 race starts, including the coveted Prince of Wales Cup. Uffa Fox also sailed her three-up in stormy conditions 100 miles (161km) across the English Channel in 27 hours to race against the French fleet in Le Havre. He won, then sailed home again in 37 hours.

*Avenger* set a pattern for many years to come. She had a fine bow with prominent V sections that developed into a flat floor aft. Carvel built, she was narrow, with a beam of just 4ft 8in (146cm), narrowing to 3ft (91cm) at the transom.

Her mast was also an advance. Up until that time, spars had been limited to 15ft 6in (475cm) in order to fit inside a standard goods wagon. The International 14 hull was the largest that could be sent by train

– which dinghy sailors did in those days to compete in other parts of the UK – for a fee of 6 shillings (30 pence) anywhere in England. It had been these size restrictions that had prevented the use of a Bermuda rig. Uffa overcame these constrictions by producing a jointed mast similar in principle to a fishing rod, with the top mast fitting into a metal sleeve – a concept revived many years later with the Laser.

*Avenger*'s real advantage was her ability to plane. While other International 14s could plane on occasion, *Avenger* would pick up her skirts and fly across the waves at the slightest provocation, and on the wind, she was just as efficient. But was *Avenger* the first planing dinghy? Almost certainly not, but she did it better than most. There is evidence to suggest that a New Zealander named JO Johnson designed and built a scow in 1896, and with minimal preparation, he lapped the fleet on his first race and had the boat home and packed away before the second boat crossed the finish line in New Zealand in the early 20th century – well before Uffa Fox popularised the concept.

Uffa Fox's *Avenger*, her crew flat out to stabilise her,
shows just why she was such an exciting boat to sail.

# 67 : Alloy mast

## 1930

Like so many innovations, it is the racing arena that brings them to the fore. The benefits of the alloy mast were first witnessed in the 1930 America's Cup when the US J-class defender *Enterprise* carried a mast made from what was then an exotic material – duralumin. This special aluminium alloy had been developed for the American aerospace industry. While all the other J-class yachts, including Britain's *Shamrock V*, had beautifully crafted but heavy wooden spars, the alloy spar on *Enterprise*, which was made with two extruded half sections fastened together with 80,000 rivets, weighed 4,000lb (1,814kg) – two-thirds that of its wooden counterpart.

The mast was largely the work of Charles Burgess, the brother of *Enterprise*'s designer William Starling Burgess who had previously worked on airship designs for the US Department of the Navy. He also developed *Enterprise*'s 'Park Avenue' alloy boom,

which had multiple transverse tracks to help control the aerofoil shape of the mainsail, instead of one longitudinal track. *Enterprise*, skippered by Harold Vanderbilt, beat Sir Thomas Lipton's Irish challenger *Shamrock V 4:0* in the 1930 America's Cup.

After the Second World War, dinghy-racing enthusiasts snapped up the relatively cheap supply of small gauge alloy tubing developed by the aerospace industry. One of these was British yachtsman Charles Currey, who originally worked for Fairey Aviation on converting the hot moulding process developed to construct wooden Mosquito airframes in order to mass-produce various dinghies. The first of these was the 12ft Uffa Fox-designed *Firefly*, which had a Reynolds tube mast with a tapered wooden top section. Soon, other classes followed the *Firefly*'s lead, including the International 14 and Albacore, also hot moulded by Fairey Marine.

The mast of the American J Class yacht
*Enterprise.* The spar was built up from plates
of Duralumin, fastened with 80,000 rivets.

# 68 : *Dorade* yacht and box

## 1930

*Dorade* is one of those wonder-racing yachts that just keeps on winning. She was one of the first yachts to be designed by American sailing doyens Olin and Rod Stephens, who founded the Sparkman & Stephens (S&S) design dynasty with yacht broker Drake Sparkman. The 52ft yawl was boat number four on the drawing board, commissioned by the brothers' father to keep his sons going during the Depression years. The dorade box, a watertight deck vent with a baffle that separated incoming air from spray, drawn up by the very practically minded Rod, was just one of many innovative ideas on the yacht.

*Dorade*'s success began with the 1931 Transatlantic Race. With Olin and Rod as co-skippers, she won the race from New York, USA, to Plymouth, UK, outright, beating many larger boats by two days on elapsed time. The family tasted victory in the Devon port again that season by winning the heavy weather Fastnet race too. The following year, she also won the Transpacific Yacht Race and finished second in the 1933 Bermuda Race. When the crew returned to New York, they were given a ticker-tape parade along Broadway. These successes set the two Stephens brothers on a meteoric rise; S&S yachts dominated the racing scene for the next 50 years.

*Dorade* was built at the Minneford Yard on City Island, New York, under the supervision of Rod Stephens who also developed her efficient rig and deck layout. Her hull design was influenced by the Six Metre day racers popular in New York at the time, with balanced ends, narrow beam, lead ballast deep in the keel and lightweight construction, with steam-bent rather than sawn frames.

In 1998, the Italian boatyard Cantiere Navale Dell'Argentario restored her and Olin Stephens flew over and joined her crew, winning two out of her three races in her first Classic Yacht regatta.

Now back in American hands, this spectacularly successful and long-lived yacht returned to San Francisco in 2013 to win the Transpacific Race that year, and was first in class in the Newport Bermuda Race the following year.

The indomitable *Dorade* in 2014 at the start of the Newport Bermuda Race. Her innovative dorade box can be clearly seen.

# 69 : Coastal Quick Release (CQR) anchor

## 1933

The anchor has been a feature of sailing the high seas ever since man made his first tentative steps out onto the water. The purpose of the anchor is to slow down the boat, and then to hold it in place on the sea or river floor. The earliest examples were simply boulders or baskets of rocks wrapped in rope and flung over the side. Later, anchors were made from iron, with 'flukes' or teeth to hold the anchor into the sand. These early anchors eventually developed into the familiar 'Admiralty pattern' anchor, with its pair of flutes set at right angles to the shank, which, scaled down, is now referred to as the Fisherman's anchor.

Some modifications were made in this period, including pivots to alleviate the effects of wind and tide, and prevent the anchor from pulling out of the sand, and the easier-to-handle-and-stow 'stockless anchor' that was almost universally adopted on larger ships. However the actual form of the anchor changed little for close to another century until mathematician Sir Geoffrey Ingram Taylor patented his Coastal Quick Release (CQR) plough anchor in 1933. This represented a major advance in anchor design, with a single fluke based on a double-bladed agricultural ploughshare, designed to dig into the ground. The shank articulates to allow some directional movement without the anchor pulling out. It is an anchor design that has become popular, particularly with cruising sailors.

This anchor has since spawned a number of innovative designs, including: the British Bruce, a 'claw' style anchor that will hold well in most seabeds; the German Bügel, with a special sharp tip for penetrating weeds and a roll bar to allow it to set correctly; the French Spade, which is far more lightweight than most comparable anchors; and recently the New Zealand Rocna anchors, designed to be stowed on a bow roller for quick release.

A CQR anchor set ready on the bow, ready to be swiftly
released when the crew needs to set anchor.

# 70 : *Popeye* the Sailor Man

## 1933

Popeye the Sailor Man began life with a bit part in Elzie Segar's comic strip *Thimble Theater*, which was initially centred around the life of the flighty Olive Oyl. But Popeye, with his pipe, bulging forearms, a spectacular uppercut and a passion for the culinary and medicinal benefits of spinach soon captured millions of fans around the world and became the strip's central character.

Popeye jumped from strip cartoon to movie screen in a 1933 Betty Boop cartoon called *Popeye the Sailor Man*, which was the first in a series produced by Fleischer Studios until 1942. The films introduced a host of new and engaging characters such as Swee'pea, J. Wellington Wimpy – a moocher with a hamburger obsession – and finally Bluto, Popeye's hard-headed antagonist with his fists of lead.

Popeye's obsession with spinach became an essential plot device in later cartoon adventures. The character has been credited with increasing consumption of spinach in the US by up to 33 per cent and even from saving the spinach industry from catastrophe during the Depression years.

In fact, the character apparently had such a positive influence on American eating habits that Crystal City – also known as the spinach capital of Texas – erected a statue to honour Elzie Segar, which made Popeye the first cartoon character to be immortalised in stone.

Popeye reaches for a can of his beloved green stuff in
a still from an unidentified *Popeye* film, c.1945.

# 71 : Boat shoes

## 1935

Topsiders or Docksides? It's the question that has plagued sailors since the two brands entered direct competition in the 1970s.

It all started in 1935 when Paul Sperry, a former seaman in the US Navy, was experimenting with non-slip shoe soles. One day, while walking his cocker spaniel, Prince, near his home in Connecticut, USA, he noticed the dog's amazing ability to run over ice without slipping. He examined the animal's paws and tried to replicate what he saw there on the soles of his shoes, by cutting a series of W-shape patterns with a penknife. And thus the first boat shoe was born.

The Topsider's improved grip and a white sole that didn't mark the deck, made the shoe an instant favourite among yachtsmen. By 1939, the US Navy had adopted the shoe as official footwear and it soon became popular among affluent students on the north-east coast, where most yachting activity was focused, and an integral part of the so-called 'Ivy League Look' of the 1950s and early 1960s.

Sebago entered the fray with its own brand of Dockside boat shoes in 1970. By the 1980s, boat shoes were back in fashion like never before, helped in no small part by prominent mentions in the best-selling *The Official Preppy Handbook* and their cameo roles in several John Hughes films. The battle of the boat shoes had begun, with newcomers Sebago setting the pace, thanks largely to high-quality materials and improved weld construction. Not only that, but they kept up their historic connection with sailors and the sea, becoming the first US company to sponsor a boat in the Observer Singlehanded Transatlantic Race (OSTAR) in 1984, and later sponsoring an America's Cup challenge in 1992. Not to be outdone, Sperry won the endorsement of legendary US sailor Dennis Conner to become the official shoe of the America's Cup in 1987.

After another period in the doldrums during the 1990s, boat shoes returned to centre stage when Californian clothes label Band of Outsiders featured Topsiders in its 2008 collection. Suddenly, boat shoes were once again on-trend, and this time Topsiders appeared to have the edge. Sperry teamed up with American clothing behemoth J.Crew, and soon celebrities such as Ellen DeGeneres, Blake Lively and Kayne West were wearing their shoes. Meanwhile, Sebago teamed up with Collete, Vane and La MJC, and the influential Duchess of Cambridge was spotted wearing their shoes. On the water, Topsiders sponsored the US Olympic and Paralympics sailing teams, while Sebago nabbed the Newport Boat Show and the World Match Racing Tour.

So, Topsiders or Docksides? In 2012, the question lost some of its sting when the giant shoe company Wolverine World Wide acquired Sperry Topsiders in a major buyout worth $1.2 billion. The other top company in its portfolio? Sebago, of course.

Deck shoes have made it into the fashion mainstream in
a way that no other sailing clothes have, except perhaps
the Breton shirt. These Docksides are 12 years old and
their owner wouldn't swap them for any other brand.

# 72 : Trapeze

## 1936

With the advent of the planing dinghy in the mid-1930s, sailors had to learn new techniques in order to sail them. The key was to keep the dinghy upright, and all manner of new hiking devices were developed in order to achieve this, from toe straps to the hiking donkey (a vertical pole that clipped on to the gunwale to give the crew the leverage to sit outboard).

It was Beecher Moore, the business partner to dinghy designer Jack Holt, who first came up with the idea of using a 'bell rope' attached to the hounds on his Thames A-class Rater for the crew to swing out on. This prompted Peter Scott and John Winter, two International 14 sailors, to consider the idea of wearing a harness that could be readily attached and detached from the wire crew support. This was developed in great secrecy with fellow International 14 sailors Charles Currey and Uffa Fox.

The first to try this new invention was Currey's wife, Bobby, crewing Charles in his father's 12m² Sharpie *Stormcock* during the 1936 season. Quite independently, others were experimenting with the same idea on M-class dinghies during the Southern Hemisphere summer in New Zealand.

The trapeze was given its first public airing in Britain during the 1938 Prince of Wales Cup series for International 14s aboard Scott's *Thunder and Lightning*. They won, with Scott and Winter alternating between helming and crewing out on the wire. The pair also won the Prince of Wales Cup race, winning by four minutes – a margin that so outclassed the fleet that the concept was then promptly banned!

The trapeze then received little further development in the Northern Hemisphere until reintroduced on the Coronet, later known as the 505, by designer John Westell, and the Ian Proctor-designed Osprey in 1954.

A number of racing classes are now reliant on the trapeze to get the most out of the boat. These include the 420, the 49er, the Flying Dutchman and racing catamarans such as the Tornado, which requires a trapeze to stop the bow digging into the water, making it liable to capsize.

Bobby Currey testing the trapeze for the first time aboard
Captain C Currey's 12m Sharpie *Stormcock* late in 1936.

# 73 : Marine plywood

## 1939

Around 3500 BC, it was the Egyptians who were first to see the structural benefits of gluing veneers of wood in a crosswise fashion to their sailing vessels, but it was in 1797 when British naval engineer Samuel Bentham patented what we now know as plywood. Fifty years later, Swedish inventor Immanuel Nobel, father of the Nobel Prize-founder Alfred Nobel, invented the rotary lathe that provided the mass production potential for composite wood.

Plywood was introduced into the United States as a general building material in 1865 and the first standard-sized 4ft x 8ft (1.2m x 2.4m) sheets were introduced in 1928.

True marine-grade plywood was first introduced in the Netherlands in 1939 by Cornelius (Kees) Bruynzeel, a door manufacturer from Zaandam, Netherlands. The threat of the Second World War had such a depressing effect that Kees began to look at alternative markets and latched on to the idea of an exterior grade for house building and boat construction using a newly developed water-resistant synthetic glue. The concept excited naval architect Ricus van de Stadt, who Bruynzeel commissioned to design the multi-chined Valk daysailer. Construction began in 1939, and these boats remain popular almost eight decades later. The daysailer also established van der Stadt as an innovative yacht designer who produced many more plywood designs.

Plywood was used to produce many items during the Second World War, from landing craft, lifeboats and the all-wood British Mosquito twin-engined fighter-bombers. After the war, plywood became the prime material feeding the explosion in growth of dinghy sailing with the introduction of the Enterprise, Gull, GP14, Wayfarer and Wanderer – all chine-shaped boats designed with plywood in mind for home construction.

The 10ft Mirror was a gunter rigged dinghy
designed in marine plywood for kit
construction by Jack Holt and Barry Bucknell.

# 74 : *Kon-Tiki*

## 1947

It is likely that the Vikings discovered the Americas long before Christopher Columbus did. They had the boats, the will and the daring. There is also evidence of them reaching as far as Newfoundland at the turn of the 11th century, and in the 1980s, a group of Norwegians got as far as Florida in a reconstructed Viking longboat.

This modern-day reconstruction was inspired by Thor Heyerdahl's *Kon-Tiki* expedition by raft across the Pacific Ocean in 1947, to show that there was no technical reason why South American Indians could not have settled in Polynesia during pre-Columbian times. Heyerdahl and a small team of fellow Norwegians and five Scandinavian friends travelled to Peru to construct, from balsa logs lashed with hemp, a 45ft (14m) indigenous raft, and on 28 April 1947, *Kon-Tiki* set sail to cross the Pacific. The crew journeyed for 101 days, covering 4,300 miles (6920km) before running onto a reef at Raroia in the Tuamotu Islands on 7 August. Thankfully they carried modern-day implements and a radio, together with 229 gallons (1,040 litres) of water and US compo rations, but also caught a plentiful number of fish en route.

Heyerdahl theorised that the original inhabitants of Easter Island were migrants from Peru, arguing that the Maoi statues resembled sculptures more typical of pre-Columbian Peru than any Polynesian designs. DNA samples taken subsequently from 23 islanders with a long lineage to the region showed that on average, they were 76 per cent Polynesian, 8 per cent Native American and 16 per cent European. This European element is likely to have occurred after the Dutch 'discovered' Easter Island in 1722. The South American component was much older, dating to between approximately 1280 and 1495, soon after the island was first colonised by Polynesians in around 1200.

Heyerdahl went on to write the bestselling book *Kon-Tiki: Across the Pacific in a Raft* and the subsequent film won an Academy Award in 1951. The original *Kon-Tiki* raft was salvaged from the reef at Raroia and is now on display in the Kon-Tiki Museum at Bygdøy in Oslo, Norway.

Thor Heyerdahl's raft *Kon-Tiki* pictured in 1947 on
her way across the Pacific Ocean to Polynesia.

# 75 : Optimist dinghy

## 1947

The US designer Clark Mills designed the Optimist dinghy in 1947 at the Clearwater Florida Optimist Service Club as an inexpensive junior primer for children. The simple pram was designed to be home-built from three sheets of plywood, and carries a spritsail rig that when dismantled, fits inside the boat so that it can be easily mounted on top of a car.

Dane Axel Damgaard introduced the Optimist design to Europe, and it soon spread across the continent and beyond to become the most popular dinghy in the world, with around 3,000 built annually, mostly in fibreglass. The design, which was standardised in 1960 and won international status in 1973, is now sailed in over 120 countries, and the Optimist is still the most popular teaching boat for young children. Its light weight (77lb/35kg), small sail and excellent stability allow it to be sailed in all wind conditions by even small and light children. The simplicity of its rig allows the young sailor to concentrate on learning about wind direction, waves and tides without having to worry about more complex manoeuvres. Its slow speed means that young and inexperienced sailors can be allowed to try sailing unaccompanied, since they will not be able to get very far. And the security of that experience makes it more likely that junior sailors will feel confident about sailing and want to try it again.

The first Optimist World Championship was held on the Hamble River in England in 1962, with children up to the age of 15 from Britain, Denmark, Sweden and West Germany competing. Today, children can compete in hundreds of different events, with classes scored according to age so that every sailor gets the chance to shine.

The class has spawned a large number of world and Olympic champions, including Briton Sir Ben Ainslie, the first sailor to win four Olympic medals. At the London Olympics in 2012, every US sailor – both skipper and crew – had begun their career in an Optimist.

A fleet of Optimists in fierce competition at the
Renaissance Reinsurance Junior Gold Cup at Bermuda's
Granaway Deep. Taking part are international sailors
from nine guest countries plus 24 Bermudians.

75 : OPTIMIST DINGHY, 1947

# 76 : Sunfish dinghy

## 1947

The Sunfish surfboard dinghy has grown to become the most prolific class, with some 300,000 boats spread across the world, made by seven different manufacturers. It was Alexander 'Al' Bryan and Cortlandt 'Cort' Heyniger from Waterbury, Connecticut, USA, who together conceived the simple design in 1947 as a way to put a sail on a surfboard. The American Red Cross had already rejected their plywood boat design for waterfront rescue surfboards.

Originally called the Sailfish, the design was modified in 1951 with the addition of a cockpit and a widening of the beam to accommodate Bryan's pregnant wife, which led to the lateen rigged, flat-decked marvel named Sunfish.

The introduction of fibreglass mass production in 1959 helped the class to spread right across the United States. While different manufacturers have introduced some variations over the years, the boats stand up well to repeated use and abuse, and it's not surprising to find a decades old Sunfish still in good shape. Given its low body profile, the boat is remarkably stable and buoyant, floats high and is unsinkable when capsized. It is also extremely responsive to direction and wind changes, to steering and the movement of the crew, making for an intense sailing experience in a small boat. It became a popular beach boat at holiday resorts, a good starter boat for children and adults alike, and was adopted by many clubs for racing. The first North American Championship was held in 1963.

In 1969, Bryan and Heyniger sold the manufacturing rights to the ten-pin bowling group AMF. It took the class to a new level, exporting the boats worldwide to the point where the Sunfish gained international class status in 1984 and the Pan American Games adopted it as a racing class in 1999. AMF sold the production rights to the class in 1985 and the design has passed through several hands since. The boats are now built alongside the Laser dinghy by Laser Performance, who have maintained the boat's original 'fun in the sun' philosophy.

A large fleet of Sunfish racing at the
Sunfish World Championship, Charleston,
South Carolina, USA in 2006.

# 77 : Terylene/Dacron sails

## 1952

Since sails have existed on sailing craft they have almost invariably been constructed of tightly woven cloth, such as hemp, linen or cotton. Until the 19th century, sailmakers traditionally used linen in their construction, but the increasing size and weight of sails soon made the material unviable and cotton became the 'cloth' of choice. Sail canvas was made from 'duck', formerly the Dutch word for cloth but now a word that has evolved to describe a particular type of cloth. These natural fibres were not ideal for sailcloth since they were vulnerable to the effects of the sun, salt and rot, but for many years there was simply no viable alternative.

The development of a strong, alternative synthetic fibre proved the catalyst for radical change in the sailmaking industry. Polyethylene terephthalate (PETE), better known under the trademark names of Terylene and Polyester film in the UK, Dacron and Mylar in the USA, and Lavsan in Russia, is one of the developmental wonders to arise during the Second World War.

The breakthrough came in 1941 from British chemists John Whinfield and James Dickson, employees of the Calico Printers' Association of Manchester, who advanced the earlier research of Wallace Carothers to produce PETE as a fibre. ICI then produced it as Terylene and Dupont, which bought the US rights, branded it as Dacron.

This man-made fibre transformed sailing, quickly superseding cotton as a sail cloth, and hemp and cotton as a key ingredient in ropes and warps. The synthetic fibre is not only stronger, waterproof and more resistant to abrasion, but it is also resistant to mould, to which cotton was always particularly susceptible. Dupont went on to develop polyester into Mylar film in 1952, which was later introduced as the outer substrate to form an even stronger sail material.

Modern racing yachts have benefitted from improvements in sail technology including ever stronger, lighter materials.

# 78 : *The Old Man and the Sea* by Ernest Hemingway

## 1952

There are few good novels about the sea but *The Old Man and the Sea* is a brilliantly evocative yarn about an aging Bahamian fisherman and his struggle to catch a giant marlin, written by the American author Ernest Hemingway.

First published in 1952, this was Hemingway's last and most celebrated work, which won him both the Nobel Prize for Literature and a Pulitzer Prize. The novel starts by telling how Santiago has gone 84 days without catching a fish, a mark of such ill-luck that the parents of his young apprentice, Manolin, forbid him from sailing with the old fisherman any more. The boy still visits Santiago's shack every night to help him with his fishing gear and to talk baseball. Santiago assures his young friend that he is about to end this unlucky streak by going far out into the Gulf Stream to fish the following day. He is rewarded by a strike so big that Santiago is unable to reel in his gear. Instead, the marlin tows his small skiff for two days and nights, and it becomes a huge battle of wills between the fish and fisherman.

On the third day, the fish begins to circle the skiff. Worn out and almost delirious, Santiago uses his last remaining strength to pull the fish onto its side and stab it with a harpoon. He then straps the marlin to the side of his boat and heads home, thinking about the high price the fish will bring him at the market and how many people he will feed.

But he had not counted on the sharks being attracted to the marlin's blood. Santiago kills one great mako with his harpoon, but loses the weapon in the process. He improvises by strapping his knife to the end of an oar to ward off further attacks and kills five more, but still the sharks keep coming. By nightfall they have devoured the marlin's entire carcass, leaving just a skeleton. Santiago finally reaches the shore, struggles back to his shack exhausted and falls into a deep sleep.

The next day a group of fishermen gather around the boat and marvel at the fish's skeleton which measures 18ft (5.5m) from nose to tail. Manolin, worried about the old man, rushes to his shack and cries upon finding him safely asleep. The book ends on an emotional note with the two promising to fish together once again.

A great yarn, well worth re-reading.

Actor Spencer Tracy (1900–1967) as Santiago talks to the marlin in a scene
from the 1958 film of *The Old Man and the Sea* based on the novella.

# 79 : Airfix model of *Golden Hind*

## 1954

Most of us have completed an Airfix model, if not for ourselves then with our children and grandchildren. Hungarian businessman Nicholas Kove founded Airfix in the UK in 1939, in order to manufacture inflatable toys. Injection moulding machines were added in 1947 to produce pocket combs, and it was quite by chance that the company moved into manufacturing kit models when Massey Ferguson commissioned Airfix to create a promotional model of a Ferguson TE20 tractor, for distribution to Ferguson sales representatives in 1949. To increase sales and lower production costs the model was later sold in kit form in Woolworths' high street stores, which took a lead role in the marketing of the kits.

Jim Russon, Woolworths' buyer, suggested to Airfix that it produce a model kit of Sir Francis Drake's galleon *Golden Hind*, best known for its global circumnavigation between 1577 and 1580. Drake's mission transformed from being one of exploration to more of piracy as he wreaked havoc against Spanish interests in South America. On his return, with a haul of Spanish gold, Queen Elizabeth I knighted Drake.

To meet Woolworths' retail price of 2 shillings (0.06p pence), Airfix packaged the product in a plastic bag with a paper header that had the assembly instructions on the reverse. Launched in 1954, the *Golden Hind* kit was a huge success and led to a wide range of detailed scale models that included famous aircraft, battle tanks and ships, notably the *Cutty Sark* clipper ship.

Airfix has had its ups and downs, but Hornby Hobbies saved the much-loved toymaker from bankruptcy in 2006, and has since relaunched many old favourites, including, of course, the *Golden Hind*.

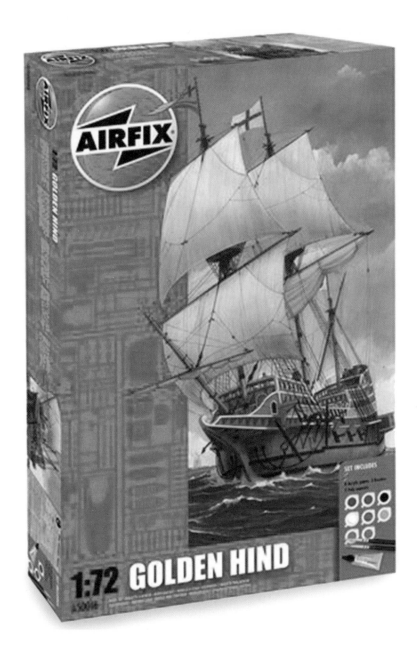

The Airfix *Golden Hind* is currently available at a 1:72 scale
which will produce a substantial finished ship. Over the years
it has been available at various scales and levels of detail.

# 80 : VHF radio

## 1960s

The very high frequency VHF radio is so commonplace on even the smallest boats that it is hard to believe it did not exist before the 1960s. In time-honoured fashion, its development came almost by accident. Following the Second World War, a new plan to introduce different wavelengths was set up across Europe, but because Germany did not exist as a state in 1948, it was not invited to the Copenhagen conference. Instead the 'country in purdah' was allocated only a small number of medium-wave frequencies that no other countries wanted because of their poor broadcasting quality. This encouraged German scientists to experiment with an ultra short-wave band, now known as VHF, which was not covered by the Copenhagen Plan.

They soon realised that FM radio with its superior sound quality, which had been introduced to Germany in 1948, was a much better alternative for VHF radio than AM. They also turned VHF's limited 'line of sight' transmission range into a positive when it was determined that transmitters placed several hundred miles apart would not interfere with each other. Soon, other European nations latched on and VHF became the norm for broadcasting local radio and TV signals.

The International Telecommunications Union then established the radio frequency range between 156.0 and 162.025MHz, exclusively as a VHF maritime mobile band to summon rescue services and communicate with harbours, locks, bridges and marinas. These frequencies operate on set channels with 16 (156.8MHz) designated as the international calling and distress channel. Transmission power ranges between 1 and 25W, giving a maximum range of up to about 60 nautical miles between aerials mounted on ships and hills, and around 5 nautical miles between aerials mounted on small boats at sea level.

Modern marine VHF radios now have a digital selective calling (DSC) facility, to allow a distress signal to be sent with a single button press that identifies the calling vessel, the nature of the emergency and the distressed vessel's position, if the radio is hooked up to a GPS receiver.

Tracy Edwards using the radio telephone on *Maiden* during
the 1989/90 Whitbread Round The World Yacht Race.

# 81 : Henri Lloyd sailing jacket

## 1963

Henri Strzelecki, a Polish refugee who arrived in Britain during the Second World War to join the Free Polish Army, settled in Manchester after hostilities ceased and became a leader of the marine and outdoor leisure-wear clothing industry. After first studying textiles at college and then gaining experience with local companies, he formed the Henri Lloyd label with Angus Lloyd in 1963 and went on to supply leading yachtsmen and mountaineers with bespoke waterproof clothing.

'Mr Henri', or 'Waterproof Henry', as he was variously known, transformed the industry with his Oxford-proofed, Bri-nylon waterproofed jackets and trousers, which outperformed and outlasted the cheaper PVC clothing available at the time. Before Strzelecki and Lloyd opened their first workshop in a converted chapel in Salford, sailing clothing had progressed little since Captain Scott's expedition to the South Pole five decades earlier.

The Henri Lloyd brand name became synonymous with sailing after Robin Knox-Johnston wore a set of Henri Lloyd waterproofs during the 1968/69 *Sunday Times* Golden Globe Race, becoming the first to sail solo non-stop around the world. Francis Chichester also wore Henri Lloyd clothing during his sailing exploits in the 1960s and 1970s, and Edward Heath and his *Morning Cloud* crews cemented Henri Lloyd's reputation by wearing their brand in major offshore races.

Henri Lloyd went on to pioneer other innovations, including the first non-corrosive zipper made of nylon, the use of Velcro closures in waterproof garments and the hand taping of seams as an alternative to varnishing. The company also pioneered the use of Gore-Tex breathable waterproof clothing during the 1980s.

Henri Strzelecki was awarded a Member of the Most Excellent Order of the British Empire (MBE) in 1985 and his company won two Queen's Awards for Export Achievement in 1986 and 1987. He died in 2012 at the age of 87 and his sons, Paul and Martin, now manage the company, which has more than 40 stores spanning Australia, Europe, the Middle East and the UK.

Wearing a Henri Lloyd jacket, Robin Knox-Johnston, the first man to sail solo non-stop around the world, waves to the crowds on his return to Falmouth, England on 22 April 1969, after completing the 30,123 mile voyage in 312 days.

# 82 : Breton/Portland course plotter

## 1964

The Breton Plotter, also known as the Portland Course Plotter, consolidates the boat, ruler, compass rose and protractor into a simple navigational instrument designed to simplify chart navigation in small yachts.

It makes child's play of converting angles from true to compass and vice versa. By reading off variation from the compass rose printed on the chart and adding or subtracting compass error from the compass deviation card, you simply revolve the plotter rose to match the combined error and read off the true or magnetic course in the centreline window. Et voila!

Captain Yvonnick Gueret, a Breton seaman whose changing fortunes led him from delivering yachts to working on small fishing boats and eventually commanding merchant vessels, invented the Breton Mk 1 Sirius Plotter. He ended his career teaching navigation, during which he realised how hard it was for students to understand how to use the esoteric plotters widely employed at the time. From this, he decided to attempt to produce a chart tool that replicated the conditions a vessel faces at sea.

The instrument was launched onto the market in 1979 and won universal approval, not least from the magazine *Yachting World*: 'The Breton plotter is one of the simplest plotters available, and as such, is easier to use in bad conditions than some of the more complicated aids.' After giving his own concise instructions for its use, the reviewer concluded, 'It takes less time to do than it does to read about it, which is probably why the Breton is so popular.'

Significantly, Gueret failed to secure a patent on his plotter, and before long a plethora of clones, including the British Portland Course Plotter, made their way onto the market.

A Breton or Portland Course Plotter enables the
navigator to plot a course using compass points.

# 83 : Perspex dome / Éric Tabarly

## 1964

The 1960s were pioneering years. The first Observer Singlehanded Transatlantic Race (OSTAR) proved that yachts could be sailed solo across oceans safely and led men like Francis Chichester, who won that event, Alec Rose and the most celebrated of them all, Robin Knox-Johnston, to complete solo circumnavigations. These pioneers captured the imagination, but no one more so than French Naval lieutenant Éric Tabarly.

Tabarly first came to prominence in 1964 when he won the second running of the OSTAR with the ketch-rigged *Pen Duick II*, a radical yacht that he had designed himself, with a clipper bow, chine sides and an engine that he fitted upside down to improve her rating. One of the many on board innovations was a Perspex dome fitted through the deck to give him 360-degree vision while helming from inside the boat with the aid of a self-steering system. Although a great idea, the remote self-steering

system failed on the eighth day, leaving Tabarly with no choice but to hand steer for the remainder of the race – 19 days with him sleeping in bursts of 90 minutes at a time. Tabarly won the race in just 27 days, 3 hours and 56 minutes, clipping 13 days off Chichester's time four years previously.

The victory turned Tabarly into an overnight hero. On his return to France, President de Gaulle made him a Chevalier de la Legion d'Honneur.

Though the use of Perspex was novel, the idea of a 360-degree viewing port on a yacht was not. Colonel Blondie Haslar, founder of the OSTAR, had a rotating canvas hood fitted in his Folkboat *Jester*, which could be turned like a deck vent away from the spray, or folded down in order to allow him to stand waist-high through the deck to adjust *Jester's* junk rig. It was this innovation that perhaps gave Tabarly the idea for a fully enclosed dome, which many endurance sailors have copied since.

Éric Tabarly in Plymouth on board *Pen Duick II* on 26 May 1964, preparing for the OSTAR. His innovative dome was yet to be fully tested.

# 84 : *Sunday Times* Golden Globe Race

## 1968/9

The *Sunday Times* Golden Globe Race was the first round-the-world yacht race and to make the challenge even tougher, it was non-stop, single-handed. Winner Robin Knox-Johnston returned to a hero's welcome at Falmouth, UK, on 22 April 1969, after spending 312 days aboard his 32ft traditional ketch *Suhaili*. The British yachtsman not only broke one of the last remaining challenges left to man but left in his wake the tales of disaster, daring and despair of eight other sailors who started this challenge but failed to finish.

The race set the foundations for the first Whitbread Round the World Race (now Volvo Ocean Race) for fully crewed yachts in 1973 and later the BOC Around Alone Race and Vendée Globe solo round-the-world races.

The rules were very simple.

Competitors had to: Embark between the months of June and October 1968 to avoid the Southern winter; sail south of all the Great Capes – Good Hope, Leeuwin and Horn; have no outside assistance or anyone board their boat during the voyage; the first to return to England from any port north of 40°N would be awarded the Golden Globe trophy and the winner on elapsed time would be awarded £5,000.

Of the nine starters, four retired before leaving the Atlantic Ocean. British yachtsmen John Ridgeway and Bill King suffered dismastings, Italian Alex Carozzo developed an ulcer and Frenchman

Loick Fougeron was forced to stop in St Helena.

Of the rest, Chay Blyth, who had little previous sailing experience, rounded the Cape of Good Hope only to pull in to East London after his yacht had suffered a succession of terrifying broaches in the Southern Ocean. Frenchman Bernard Moitessier got as far as Cape Horn and looked likely to overhaul front-runner Robin Knox-Johnston to become both first and fastest home, then messaged that he was going to continue on around the Southern Ocean – 'to save my soul' – and continued on past the Cape of Good Hope before finally throwing down his anchor in a Tahiti lagoon.

British entrant Donald Crowhurst set out from Teignmouth in some disarray on 31 October, the final day, and quickly realised that his trimaran *Teignmouth Electron* would not survive the rigours of the Southern Ocean. He was soon wrestling with the idea of whether to accept defeat or remain in the Atlantic and spin a yarn about sailing around the globe. On 6 December, he made up his mind to cheat and two days later won a fanfare of publicity after claiming a Noon-to-Noon solo record of 243 miles. In reality, he achieved only 170.

Once Knox-Johnston had returned to Falmouth to win the *Sunday Times* Golden Globe trophy, Crowhurst 'reappeared' on 4 May and began to chase Nigel Tetley in his trimaran, *Victress*, in earnest. His fictitious voyage through the Southern Ocean

Robin Knox-Johnston on board his 32ft (9.8m) boat
*Suhaili*, in the Atlantic near the end of his
circumnavigation of the earth.

suggested that *Teignmouth Electron* reached the Horn some two weeks ahead of Tetley's elapsed time. This forced Tetley to push even harder but his trimaran was in no state to be pressed. Her floats were leaking badly, the outer skin of fibreglass sheathing was peeling off, and on 30 May, just 1,200 miles (1,931km) from the finish, her port float broke completely and smashed into the main hull. Tetley watched from his life raft as his trimaran sank. At the time, Crowhurst was still in the Southern Hemisphere, midway up the Brazilian coast. If he had planned to come in a close second to Tetley and

share in the glory without having his logs scrutinised, the demise of *Victress* put the spotlight squarely on *Teignmouth Electron*. The closer he got towards the Western Approaches, the more distressed Crowhurst became, and on 1 July, he is thought to have jumped overboard in the mid-Atlantic, 1,200 miles (1,931km) west of Madeira, unable to live with the deception he had started.

Knox-Johnston, being the only finisher out of the nine entries, won both the Golden Globe and the £5,000, but donated his winnings to Crowhurst's widow and her four children.

# 85 : First sailing hydrofoil

## 1969

People have been experimenting with hydrofoils since 1898 when Italian inventor Enrico Forlanini came up with his 'ladder' foil system to lift a motorboat hull clear of the water. British designer and inventor, John Thornycroft, constructed a series of boat models to test his theories between 1899 and 1901, and in 1909, built the 22ft (6.7m) *Miranda III*, which had a foil to raise its bow clear of the water. Her successor, *Miranda IV*, set a top speed of 35 knots.

In the US, Alexander Graham Bell, inventor of the telephone, was also intrigued by the idea of flying a hull on hydrofoils clear of the water. His HD-4 powerboat reached a speed of 61.57 knots in 1919 – a world record that stood for two decades. After the Second World War, Russia and Italy led the world in developing passenger and military hydrofoil craft.

Not until 1969 did British sailor James Grogono adapt a two-man Tornado catamaran to become the first to fly a sailboat on hydrofoils. Aptly named *Icarus*, her wooden foils proved both heavy and fragile, and it was not until he developed metal foils that her full potential was realised. During the 1972 Weymouth Sailing Speed Week, *Icarus* reached an average speed of 21.5 knots over a 1,640ft (500m) course, and improved in small increments over the next 15 years to reach a B-class record of 28.4 knots.

The first sailing monohull to ride on hydrofoils was an International Moth, built by Frank Raison in 1974, but it was not until 2001 that Australian Brett

Burvill perfected the concept sufficiently to beat a standard Moth right around a race course at the Moth World Championships in Australia. Rohan Veal went on to win the world championship in 2005. His performance transformed the class, and now all competitive International Moths are foil-borne.

Inl 1984 people began to experiment with foils on offshore racing boats. French sailor Éric Tabarly was the first, with his 60ft foil-assisted trimaran *Paul Ricard*. He finished fourth in the 1984 Observer Singlehanded Transatlantic Race (OSTAR), but then on the return voyage, smashed the west–east transatlantic record set by the schooner *Atlantic* 75 years earlier.

Tabarly continued to experiment with hydrofoils, and with fellow Frenchman Alain Thébault, built and tested a one-third-scale model of a foil-borne trimaran in 1987, which later became known as *l'Hydroptère*. It took another seven years before these ideas were realised in full scale and another decade to develop this vessel's full potential.

In 2005, *l'Hydroptère* established a cross-Channel sailing record from Dover to Calais. In 2009, she set an outright sailing speed record of 51.36 knots across a 1,640ft (500m) distance, and averaged 50.17 knots over 1 nautical mile. In 2013, she became the first foiling sailboat to cross the Pacific from Long Beach, California, to Hawaii, but light winds thwarted their attempt to break the sailing record.

The foil-borne offshore trimaran *l'Hydroptère*,
skippered by Alain Thibault set a world record speed
of 44.5 knots over 500 metres and 41.5 knots over one
nautical mile in 25 knot north-east winds.

85 : FIRST SAILING HYDROFOIL, 1969

# 86 : Windsurfer

## 1970

Who invented the Windsurfer? Not Hoyle Schweitzer and fellow Californian Jim Drake, who claimed the first patent for a sailboard they trademarked as the Windsurfer. They based their design on an idea Newman Darby first conceived in 1948 for a handheld sail and rig mounted on a universal joint, which he found allowed him to steer a conventional 3m-long sailboat without a rudder, by tipping the rig forward to bear away, and aft to turn up into the wind.

Schweitzer began mass-producing polyethylene sailboards to their Windsurfer design in 1970 and saw the sport explode right across America and Europe, to the point where one in every three households that owned a boat also had a sailboard.

The first Windsurfing World Championship was held in 1973 and sailboarding became an Olympic sport for men in 1984, and for women in 1992. Throughout this time Schweitzer controlled his patent ferociously, claiming large damages from any who refused to buy a licence.

One company to fall foul of this litigiousness was the French manufacturer Tabur Marine, owned by Baron Bich, of Bic pen fame. The company mass-produced all manner of small boats including a sailboard, using polypropylene injection moulding machines. At the court hearing in London, Tabur's lawyers centred their defence on the boyhood creation of Peter Chilvers, who, in 1958, at the age of 12, had assembled a rudder-steered board powered by a sail in Chichester Harbour, years before Windsurfing International had filed a patent for the Windsurfer. Although the Chilvers sailboard differed in significant respects from the Windsurfer, including the use of a rudder for steering, the court ruled for Tabur, blowing Hoyle Schweitzer's claims to worldwide royalties.

Chilvers went on to become a successful engineer working directly with Colin Chapman at Lotus Cars and later founded a sailing and windsurfing centre in London for disadvantaged children. But he never made any money from the sailboard principle.

The simplest idea has created a hugely pleasurable
sport – perhaps best enjoyed in sunshine and a
warm sea – but also exhilarating in stronger wind.

**86 : WINDSURFER, 1970**

# 87 : WEST system epoxy

## 1970

Epoxy resin is another wonder-product to emerge from the Second World War, but it took three decades for it to permeate down to mainstream boat construction. Its pioneers were the Gougeon Brothers, Meade and Jan, from Michigan, USA, who were first to see the possibilities of the material in 1958, when patternmakers started to use epoxy formulations to glue wooden shapes together.

In 1960, Meade built two cold-moulded wooden boats using epoxy as the adhesive, followed by his first trimarans, built with his brother Jan in Pennsylvania. These early experiments led to mixed results, most notably epoxy's early limitations as a coating material. What encouraged them to continue was the glue's ability to bond different materials together, as well as its high moisture-resistance.

Returning to their hometown, Bay City, Michigan, the two brothers bought a boatyard to build lightweight iceboats and experiment with epoxy formulations. The breakthrough came in 1970 when they developed an epoxy resin that could easily be applied both as a glue to bond wood veneers together and as a moisture barrier over wood, metal and fibreglass. The Gougeon Brothers' Boatworks rapidly expanded, and by 1973, it was the largest builder of iceboats on either side of the Great Lakes.

Many people who saw the iceboats were interested in using Gougeon Brothers' epoxy system for their own building and repair projects, so by 1971, the brothers were selling epoxy systems to other boatbuilders and sailing enthusiasts. By 1973, the Gougeons began to expand into other boat-building projects, developing their resin system's trade named as WEST epoxy, which became a popular choice for making fibreglass repairs, too.

During the 1970s, the Gougeon Brothers built several high-profile offshore racing boats, including *Adagio*, a 35ft wooden trimaran, which is still sailing today. Another was the Ron Holland-designed 2-tonner *Golden Dazy*, which won the Canada's Cup in 1975, followed by Phil Weld's Dick Newick-designed 60ft trimaran *Rogue Wave*, which won the 1976 Observer Singlehanded Transatlantic Race, and *Patient Lady*, a C-class catamaran that went on to win the 1977 Little America's Cup. The success of these wood/epoxy composite boats led other builders and designers to appreciate that they too could build stiffer, stronger hulls with WEST epoxy.

In 1979, NASA approached the Gougeon Brothers to produce experimental wood/epoxy wind turbine blades, which led to multi-million dollar contracts to manufacture 4,300 blades between 1979 and 1993. This gave the brothers the money to fund further research into developing extremely lightweight structures, improve the performance of their WEST system and market the resin worldwide.

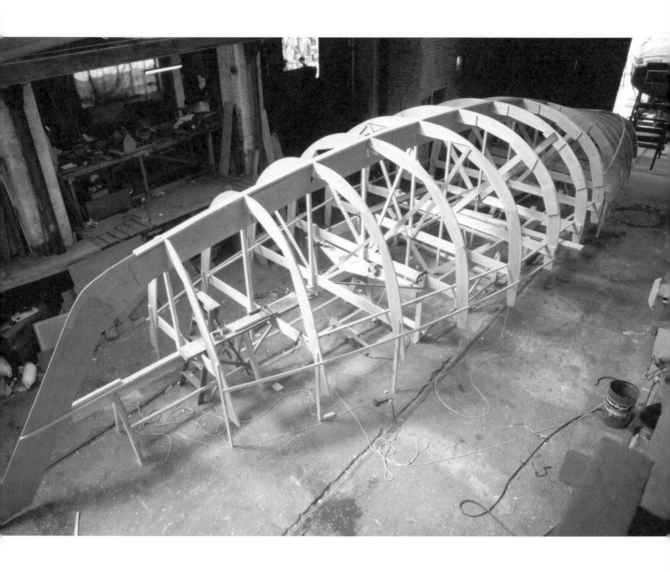

The wooden hull of this yacht is ready for the cold-moulding

process and will be bonded using the WEST system epoxy,

to create a watertight finish and smooth profile.

# 88 : Sunsail flotilla, first flotilla charter

## 1975

It was an airline pilot who first had the idea of setting up group sailing holidays in the Sun. John Charnley was flying VC10s (a long-range British airliner) when the British Overseas Airways Corporation (BOAC) merged with British European Airways (BEA) to form British Airways (BA) in 1974, He soon became disillusioned with the union disputes and political infighting of the newly formed company. Flying was expensive in those days, and when Britain was hit by a rush on the pound during the 'sterling crisis', as it was known, the government decided to limit the amount a traveller could take aboard to just £30.

This was the catalyst that led to a new generation of young entrepreneurs creating the 'package holiday', a type of all-inclusive tour overseas where holidaymakers bought their flights, transfer, hotel, food and often drinks as part of the package, paid in sterling in the UK. This circumnavigated the limitations on would-be travellers taking money overseas and led to a whole new industry, as revolutionary as the 'no-frills' airlines of today.

Pilot John Charnley was the first to realise that while air transit package holidays were, quite literally, taking off, nobody was doing the same for sailing. A keen yachtsman himself and aware of the allure of the Greek Islands, he started the company that became Sunsail while still flying BA planes. Within a year, his concept of offering sailing-in-company flotilla holidays in Greek waters, with or without a skipper, proved so appealing that he handed in his wings within a year. He then worked to expand the business into what is now the largest yacht charter and watersports company in the world, with more than 800 yachts across 30 locations throughout the Caribbean, Mediterranean, South Pacific, Indian Ocean and Europe.

Charnley eventually sold the business to one of the world's most successful beer brands, Guinness, in 1998, and Sunsail is now a part of the TUI Travel empire.

Today, holidaymakers have a huge choice of yachting holidays open to them. They can hire an experienced skipper to show them the ropes for a few days or for the entire trip, they can charter their own yacht and make their own itinerary, or they can join a flotilla in the Greek Islands as Charnley originally envisaged, and now do the same in the Virgin Islands, Croatian waters and around the Turkish coast.

A flotilla of Sunsail yachts making the most of a perfect sea. Sailing in company allows the novice sailor to gain experience with help nearby and enjoy company beyond the confines of the boat.

# 89 : Freeze-dried food (Whitbread Race)

## 1977

It may not be haute cuisine, but freeze-dried food has been the staple diet for offshore and ocean racing crews ever since Dutchman Cornelis 'Conny' van Rietschoten first subjected his *Flyer* crew to this lightweight food source in order to win the 1977/8 Whitbread Round the World Race.

Van Rietschoten had just sold his electrical contractor business and at the age of 49 was looking for fresh challenges. He had not raced since competing in the 1953 Fastnet Race, so he entered the Whitbread Race with a competitive but open mind. When considering how to feed his crew, he immediately saw the advantage of freeze-dried food, which provides an 80 per cent weight-saving advantage over fresh stores and even more over tinned food. It can also be placed anywhere in the boat without affecting trim, while the fresh water required is stored in tanks directly above the keel, where it adds to stability.

Freeze drying is an almost instant process; the food is first frozen before the water content is evaporated away under vacuum, ensuring that both flavour and nutrients are retained.

The Dutch skipper spent three days sampling this space-age powdered fare at a US laboratory with the head dietician from Martinaire, the Netherlands' leading airline caterers, tasting all manner of dishes, from Shrimp Creole to Mexican omelette before drawing up a series of menus on a seven-day cycle in order to provide his crew with the correct balance of calories, minerals and vitamins.

Did it help them win? There were complaints that one meal tasted very much like the next, whatever it said on the packet, but van Rietschoten persevered with the products and, four years later, became the only skipper to win two Whitbread Round the World races.

Freeze-dried food is now widely used in round-the-world yacht races and by those undertaking solo sailing and rowing adventures, in order to reduce the weight of stores carried because of its excellent nutrition per gram of weight.

Tony Mutter (right) of New Zealand and his watch take
their breakfast of freeze-dried food on the Swedish
Whitbread 60 *Swedish Match* during the first leg of the
Whitbread Round the World Race 1997–98.

89 : FREEZE DRIED FOOD (WHITBREAD RACE), 1977

# 90 : Argos / EPIRB distress system

## 1978

The Argos satellite tracking system was a French Space Agency (CNES)-initiative developed during the 1970s alongside the US Space Agency, NASA and the US National Oceanic and Atmospheric Administration (NOAA). Its first use was to track 200 weather buoys drifting around the Antarctic and monitor atmospheric pressure, sea surface temperature and, by default, the direction and speed of the sea currents. The service was launched in 1978 and quickly led to the development of other scientific and sporting projects, tracking everything from mammals to yachts.

The first sailing event to use Argos was the French-run Transat en Double in 1979, quickly followed by the Observer/Europe Singlehanded Transatlantic Race from Plymouth to Newport, Rhode Island, USA, a year later. Each yacht was fitted with a small, automatic, self-powered transmitter attached to the deck. These signals, which gave position, speed and course steered, were then relayed from a US tracking station to the Argos headquarters in France and onwards to the race organisers in Plymouth. This enabled Race HQ to monitor the entire fleet on a regular basis and also provided an additional safety feature, with each unit having a manual switch that could be operated by the sailor to indicate an emergency.

Early issues with the transmitter failing due to their plastic casings cracking, allowing water to get into the works were soon resolved, and the Argos system became the standard method for tracking yachts throughout the 1980s and 1990s, until cheaper GPS systems could provide the same information on a continuous basis.

Today, a basic EPIRB can be bought for as little as £375 and one with built-in GPS just a little more. They can also be activated either manually or automatically when the EPIRB comes into contact with water. Manual activation brackets cover the water sensors, preventing them from activating the EPIRB if, for example, a wave breaks over the boat, and keeping it to hand should access be required. Auto Float-free housings automatically deploy the EPIRB when it is submerged deeper than 6.5–13ft (2–4m) in the sea when a hydrostatic release cuts the EPIRB free from its housing, causing it to activate. Hundreds of sailors are rescued annually as a result of this technology.

An EPIRB of the kind carried on a boat: they can be used anywhere in the world and once activated will transmit for a minimum of 48 hours. An EPIRB is registered to a vessel which means that if you have an EPIRB and buy a new yacht you will need to re-register it when installing in your new boat.

# 91 : *Assent* – Fastnet survivor

## 1979

The 1979 Fastnet Race was the worst disaster in the history of offshore racing. Of the 303 starters in this 605-mile (974km) classic event from Cowes out to the Fastnet Rock and back to Plymouth, only 86 finished. The Atlantic storm that thrashed the fleet led to 18 fatalities (15 yachtsmen and three rescuers), causing 24 crews to abandon ship and 100 or more reported knockdowns. In total, 77 yachts were rolled at least once in the mountainous waves.

In among these stories of unprecedented carnage were several superlatives. Peter Blake and his crew aboard the 77ft maxi yacht *Condor of Bermuda* revelled in the conditions. The team rounded the Fastnet 90 minutes ahead of their nearest rivals aboard *Kialoa*, and smashed the race record by nearly eight hours. Ted Turner, the flamboyant founder of the US broadcaster CNN, won the race on handicap with his yacht *Tenacious*.

Another was the remarkable story of *Assent*, a Contessa 32 – one of the smallest yachts in the race – sailed by the 23-year-old Alan Ker and four young friends, all aged between 18 and 25 and all experienced offshore sailors. They were aware that the seas were large but were not unduly worried. Soon they began to pass yachts that had turned over or were hove-to. They then caught the brunt of the storm, suffering two knockdowns, one beyond horizontal. However, given the extreme roughness of the seas and despite losing radio contact, they decided to hold their course to Fastnet rather than turning back. Alan and his crew remained largely unaware of the disaster unfolding around them until they arrived at Millbay Dock in the middle of the night to find the place almost deserted. They were the only finisher in their class and won the respect of the sailing community for managing to survive the terrible conditions.

*Assent*'s amazing resilience encouraged Alan's father, Willie Ker, to use the vessel to circumnavigate Iceland, sail to Greenland and Baffin Island, and cruise to the Antarctic and up to Alaska and Russia, voyages that he undertook alone on the whole, secure in the ability of the yacht to survive anything the high seas could throw at her.

Following her sturdy performance in the Fastnet
Race, *Assent* has had many further adventures.
Here she is shown on one of her polar voyages.

# 92 : *Colt Cars* – first carbon fibre vessel

## 1982

The 1980s was an explosive era for all manner of marine innovation, and the use of exotic building materials, such as Kevlar – a fibre of high tensile strength used to add strength to materials as diverse as rubber and nylon – and carbon fibre, headed the list. The first to take advantage of this miracle in aerospace technology was New Zealand yacht designer Ron Holland and British round-the-world yachtsman Rob James, who enjoyed the financial backing of Japanese conglomerate Mitsubishi, manufacturers of Colt cars. Together, they embarked on building a 60ft state-of-the-art trimaran to counter French dominance in offshore multihull racing, by employing Kevlar and carbon fibre in the moulding of *Colt Cars GB*.

The trimaran had a chequered career. Rob, sailing with his wife Naomi James, won the 1982 Binatone two-man Round Britain Race in the record time of 16 days, but minor gear breakages in other races led to more retirements than finishes.

The lowest point came in March 1983 when James slipped and fell through the safety netting strung between hulls while entering Salcombe Harbour. *Colt Cars GB* did not have an engine, and the three other crew on board struggled to turn the boat back in time to save James from dying of hypothermia.

During the mid-1980s, sailing enthusiast Don Wood reincarnated the boat, rechristening her *Red Star Night Star*, and went on to enjoy some success with her.

Years later the boat received a new lease of life as *Spirit of Ireland* when raced by Rob Deasy in the 1992 Europe 1 STAR Transatlantic Race. Sadly, the boat's ill luck continued, for she collided with a ship and was left abandoned in the mid-Atlantic. Fifty-seven days later, the trimaran drifted up on Flores in the Azores and was salvaged and refurbished. She then set off on a global circumnavigation in 2005 and was last seen in East Asian brokerage adverts in 2014, with an asking price of $201,672.

Rob James and Naomi James sailing *Colt Cars GB*.
Despite the radical design of her triple hulls her racing
performance did not match her design innovations.

# 93 : Solar shower bag

## 1980s

Keeping clean on board a small boat has always been a tricky proposition and it's undoubtedly true that for years many sailors got away with the minimum, taking a full shower or bath only when they were in harbour. Yet despite this, the solar shower is such a simple gadget that you are left wondering why it took until the 1980s to invent it. When used in warmer climates, this clever device has proved a real boon for sailors and campers alike.

In its simplest form, the easily transportable solar-powered shower consists of a black PVC bag holding 5 gallons (19 litres) of water and a flexible plastic tube to direct the hot water where you want it to go – in other words, a simplified form of shower head. A hook allows you to position the bag in the most convenient position for showering. It is then operated by filling the bag with water and hanging it in the rigging or from a tree branch by the beach. Then you simply wait two to three hours for the Sun's rays to heat the water to around 43 degrees Celsius (110 degrees Fahrenheit), before you have yourself a glorious mobile shower – much appreciated after long months at sea. Some of the more sophisticated models even have a built-in temperature strip that lets you know when the water has reached the required temperature.

The shower is ideal for sailing in the Tropics, but the system will also take the chill off cold water on cloudy days. You can also add hot water from a kettle to help it to heat more quickly. Far more civilised than a cold seawater shower, and for as little as £6, they are a cheap and effective means of keeping clean on board.

The solar shower bag can be hung anywhere
there is a place for a hook and left to warm up
in the sunshine for a refreshing shower.

# 94 : *Australia II* yacht

## 1983

*Australia II* (KA 6) is the wing-keeled wonder yacht that famously ended the New York Yacht Club's 132-year tenure of the America's Cup. The radical 12m yacht was designed by Ben Lexcen for Alan Bond's Royal Perth Yacht Club challenge in 1983, and was skippered by John Bertrand.

The 12m rule that governed the America's Cup class yachts balances waterline length against sail area: the longer the waterline (a speed benefit), the smaller the sail area. *Australia II*'s short chord winged keel gave the boat a significant advantage in manoeuvrability and because of its lower centre of gravity, a much-improved righting moment over standard fin keel yachts.

Lexcen drew a hull very close to the minimum 44ft allowance, which enabled him to maximise on sail area and take full advantage of the greater stability of his wing keel. The whole package was a major design advance and the yacht dominated the Louis Vuitton challenger trials, culminating with a 4–1 defeat over Britain's *Victory 83* in the finals.

By now, the New York Yacht Club America's Cup Committee was alert to the very real threat *Australia II* posed to Dennis Conner's *Liberty*, which had won the defence trials, and New York YC America's Cup committee members went out of their way to have *Australia 2* eliminated by any means possible. First, they tried to purchase the keel design from the Netherlands Ship Model Basin, the tank

testing facility in which Lexcen had perfected his design. When that failed, the Committee tried to rule *Australia II*'s wing keel as a 'peculiarity' and as such illegal under the 12m rule. The Australians might have come unstuck here, for they had not requested an official interpretation from the International Yacht Racing Union, the governing body of the sport. But Peter de Savary's *Victory* team had, and the British waived the confidentiality surrounding this ruling to prove the wing keel concept had already been ruled to be legal.

With just two weeks before the start of the Cup match, the New York Yacht Club then questioned the nationality of *Australia II*'s design. The rule governing the America's Cup at the time insisted that the designer had to be a national of the challenging country. Lexcen was certainly Australian, but what part had the scientists at the Netherlands Ship Model Basin played in the design of the wing keel? The New York Committee had secretly sent a lawyer to the Netherlands to investigate, where he had learned the key roles that Dr Peter van Oossanen (the head of the tank testing facility) and, more pertinently, Joop Sloof from the Dutch Aerospace Laboratory (who had been working on winglets for Boeing aircraft at the time) had been the ones to perfect the wing keel concept. The problem for the Americans was that neither scientist was prepared to sign an affidavit to confirm this,

Tank test model of *Australia 2* designed by Ben
Lexcen, at the Dutch tank test facility.

and without that proof, Australia's right to challenge for the Cup in *Australia II* was upheld.

During a tightly fought best-of-seven match for the America's Cup that captured the world's attention, *Australia II* defeated Dennis Conner's American defender *Liberty* 4–3 to break the longest run in sporting history.

It was much later that the truth prevailed, and by that time, the Cup had gone Down Under. It was Dr Peter van Oossanen who spilled the beans during the 1987 America's Cup held at Fremantle, western Australia. Van Oossanen claimed in an interview with *The Times* that Lexcen had tested a wide variety of ideas including a model with a standard keel fitted upside down to the tank test model. This showed some promise, offering greater stability, but created appalling turbulence around the bottom edge.

Ben went home to Australia and Peter took up the idea with Sloof, who provided van Oossanen with the information to develop winglets to provide an endplate effect on the bottom of the keel that smoothed out the flow of water. By the time Ben returned to the Netherlands, the idea had been tested and proved.

Both John Bertrand and *Australia II*'s project manager John Longley refute this side of the story, but significantly, neither they nor Alan Bond had any inkling about the wing keel until August 1981, when all the design work had been completed. In his book *Born to Win*, Bertrand recalls the shock of seeing Ben Lexcen's plans for the first time. 'I nearly flipped. After all that I had told him – no gambles, no risks, no trick boats, just put me in there on equal terms – Benny turns up with something that looks like a bloody rocket underneath my cockpit.'

Lexcen, who died in 1988 and used humour to deflect any accusations, said 'I have in mind to admit it all to the New York Yacht Club that I really owe the secret of the design to a Greek guy who helped me out and was invaluable. He's been dead for 2000 years. Bloody Archimedes ...'

*Australia II* skippered by John Bertrand, winner of the America's Cup off Newport Rhode Island in 1983.

# 95 : *Crédit Agricole*/Open 60 yacht

## 1983

Philippe Jeantot, and by default French bank Crédit Agricole, are the fallen stars in French yachting circles. The former deep-sea diver first came to prominence in 1982 when he took on the first edition of the BOC Around Alone Race, a solo circumnavigation starting from Newport, Rhode Island, with stops at Cape Town, Sydney and Rio de Janeiro before returning to the US port the following year. Jeantot's planning, preparation and attention to detail and knowledge gained from working as a diver in the oil industry, set him apart from the rest, and his yacht *Crédit Agricole II*, sponsored by the French bank, won every leg.

The Frenchman returned for the second edition of the BOC Around Alone in 1986/7 with C*rédit Agricole III*, one of the first Open 60-class yachts, which, like the previous *Crédit Agricole*, was designed by Philippe Ribadeau Dumas. Jeantot did not dominate in quite the same manner, for others were also competing with boats designed to this new 60ft singlehanded racing class rule, but his diligence and detail won through in the end.

This second victory made Jeantot a household name in France and established the Open 60 as the de facto big boat class in all solo and short-handed ocean racing events. The Frenchman, who was first inspired to take up sailing in his twenties after reading Bernard Moitessier's book, *The Long Way*, went on to found the Vendée Globe non-stop round-the-world singlehanded race in 1989, now the world's leading solo circumnavigation event raced solely in Open 60 yachts. However, he then fell from grace after being found guilty of tax evasion.

Unlike Jeantot, the Open 60-class continues to thrive both in numbers and technology, the latest boats being moulded in carbon fibre, carrying complex keels that can be swung up to windward to reduce heeling, and a cloud of sail that would have been impossible for one person to control when the class was formed three decades ago.

*Credit Agricole III* in action. She was one of the first
of the still-thriving Open 60 class that has included
yachts such as *Aviva* in which Dee Caffari competed
in the Vendée Globe and Barcelona World Races.

# 96 : Dyneema® rope

## 1990

Dyneema®, or Spectra as it is known in many parts of the world, is one of those miracle man-made space-age fibres, with a strength-to-weight ratio 15 times higher than steel. Unlike other polymer fibres, Dyneema® has a very low melting point (130 degrees Celsius/266 degrees Fahrenheit), is as slippery as Teflon and is light enough to float.

In 1963, Dutch scientist Albert Pennings invented the complex polymer chain that makes up Dyneema®, but the material did not become commercially available until 1990. It has replaced rod and wire rigging on racing yachts and in 2007, was used for the 18-mile (30km) space tether carried aboard the ESA/Russian Young Engineers' Satellite 2 programme in 2007. In the 2013 America's Cup, *Oracle Team USA* won the series in an AC72 catamaran rigged with Dyneema®.

The material has also replaced Kevlar as a protective weave in personal and vehicle armour, bowstrings, retrieving lines on spear guns and rigging lines on kites and parachutes. Its one drawback is its poor knot-holding ability. Dyneema®'s high lubricity means that ends must be spliced, which limits the material to fixed length rigging applications within the sport of sailing. But Dyneema® is so strong that it is used for the mooring ropes on two of the world's largest cruise liners, the *Oasis of the Seas* and the *Allure of the Seas*, each weighing approximately 110,000 tons (100,000 metric tonnes), with 16 passenger decks and a carrying capacity of 8,000 people. A conventional mooring rope for such a large ship would have been impossibly heavy and bulky but the strength of Dyneema® means that the ships can be held fast with a far smaller cable.

Dyneema® is incorporated into a huge range of specs
and qualities of rope. The rope pictured is for racing
yachts and features a high-performance 12 strand pu
coated Dyneema® SK78 core, which is very strong,
low stretch, lightweight and easy to splice.

# 97 : GPS

## 1990

For centuries the toughest problem confronting sailors was to figure out where they were on the high seas. Fortunes and lives were spent to find a way to fix a vessel's position. Even when the solution was finally found (see Harrison's clock, page 70), navigators had to master the art of using a sextant and going through complex mathematical formulas to arrive at their position. Then, almost overnight, an electronic gizmo was developed that told them their position in a matter of seconds.

Global Positioning System (GPS) technology was developed by the US Navy in the 1950s and 1960s, and was facilitated by the space technology developed for espionage during the Cold War. The instrument picks up signals from satellites in space and works out how far away they are, based on how long their signals take to travel from the satellite to Earth. By cross-referencing the signals from three or more satellites, it can work out where it is positioned.

The first system, using just five satellites, was trialled in 1960. In 1973 the modern system of multiple orbiting satellites was devised. Ten prototype satellites were launched between 1978 and 1985, all intended for military use, but when a Korean airliner carrying 269 passengers was shot down after straying into Soviet airspace in 1983, US President Ronald Reagan gave the go-ahead for GPS to be developed for civilian use as 'a common good'.

Between 1989 and 1994, some 24 satellites were launched for the new system, at a cost of $5 billion, and a satellite navigation system available to all finally became a global reality. It turned out to be far more accurate than the US Navy had anticipated – to within 65–98ft (20–30m) rather than the expected 328ft (100m). Concerned that enemies could use the technology to locate US targets, they inserted a deliberate error into the civilian version, which limited its accuracy to 100ft (so-called Selective Availability, or SA), while encrypted instruments used the more accurate version. The idea backfired during the 1990/1 Iraq War, when US soldiers were often issued with the more easily available civilian GPS, and found themselves at a self-imposed disadvantage. Meanwhile, several rival systems were invented to circumvent SA, and it was finally turned off by Presidential decree in 2000.

For sailors, the arrival of GPS was revolutionary. No longer would their lives depend on an instrument invented when the United States was still a colony and nor would they need to make the long calculations to convert sun and star sights into latinudal and longitudinal positions. When Garmin showed its first marine GPS in 1990, it caused a sensation and, despite the $2,500 price tag, led to a backlog of 5000 orders. By May 2014, the company had sold more than 126 million devices, and the cheapest hand-held GPS cost less than $100.

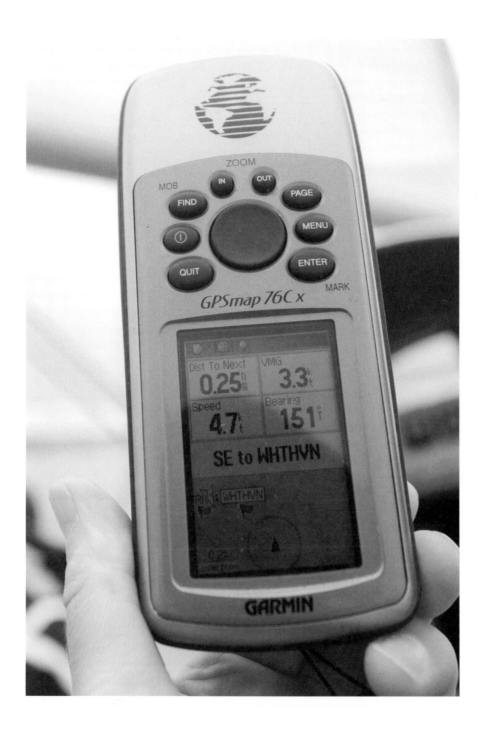

A sailor using a hand-held GPS to check his
position relative to the nearest harbour.

# 98 : *Father's Day* – smallest boat to cross the Atlantic

## 1993

The word 'can't' is not one that comes easily to American pilot Hugo Vihlen. Once he gets an idea into his head, he's like a dog with a bone; he just never gives up. Take sailing across the Atlantic in the smallest boat. He first had the idea back in 1968, but it took three madcap attempts over as many decades to beat the best efforts of the US Coastguard to save him from himself, and the worst that the weather could throw before he finally made the record books by sailing the smallest boat across the Atlantic in 1993.

Vihlen's adventures began on 29 March 1968, when he set out from Casablanca, Morocco, bound for Florida, USA, in his 5ft 11in sailboat *April Fool*. He got to within sight of the city lights of Miami on the night of 20 June after 84 days at sea, only to find that offshore winds and the Gulf Stream pushed him back. The US Coastguard launched a search at the request of his parents, and after Vihlen refused to accept a tow from other passing boats, he was forcibly picked up by the Coastguard cutter *Cape Shoalwater* the following day.

The Coastguard also thwarted Vihlen's next attempt when it refused to allow him to set sail from Cape Cod bound for England in his 5ft 6in boat *Father's Day*. Undeterred, the former fighter pilot, who had seen action during the Korean War, simply decamped to St John's, Newfoundland, where the distance to the UK was shorter, the currents ran in his favour and, most importantly, the US Coastguard was absent. This third attempt was thwarted by light, variable winds and the fact that rival yachtsman Tom McNally was competing for the same 'smallest boat' record in a vessel 1.5in (3.8cm) shorter than *Father's Day*.

So he went home and took a chainsaw to the back of his boat, reduced her length to 5ft 4in, and returned to St John's in 1993, this time making it to Falmouth, England, in 115 days. He carried rations to last only 85 days and was forced to stretch his supplies – 65 ready meals, 34 gallons (155 litres) of water, 2 gallons (9 litres) of M&Ms, a gallon of dry fruit, and 100 cans of Hawaiian Punch – to cover the four-month voyage. Explaining the choice of name for his boat, Vihlen said, 'On *Father's Day* you should be able to do what you want to do, that's your thing. This was my thing and aboard *Father's Day* I was able to do it.'

Jenny Wittamore, assistant curator at the National
Maritime Museum at Falmouth in Cornwall, inspects
*Father's Day* at the museum store and warehouse. Its
tiny size can be seen relative to a standard sized canoe.

# 99 : Camcorder

## 2001

It was Clare Francis who first made use of a 'fly on the cabin wall' camera during the 1976 Observer Singlehanded Transatlantic Race. Her tearful, emotion-charged pieces to camera exposed the true mental and physical hardships that solo sailors endure, and when the documentary on the race was aired on the BBC, it made her a national figure.

The change from cine film to video to digital, and the rapid advances in camcorder technology, have now made it possible for any number of 'flies on the wall' to transmit pictures live to TV stations and computer screens around the world.

It all began when Sony introduced the Betacam TV recording system in 1982, followed a year later with the first compact consumer camcorder. Sony was also at the forefront of digital technology with the Sony D1, which recorded uncompressed data and required a large bandwidth in order to transmit.

The big breakthrough came in 1995 when Sony, JVC and Panasonic launched the DV format, which became the standard for home video production, independent filmmaking and news reporting. This was followed by the introduction of high definition video (HDV) by Panasonic in 2000, but it was Sony, JVC, Canon and Sharp that brought prices down to levels that were affordable for many people with the launch of MiniDV cassettes in 2003. The same year Sony introduced the first tapeless camcorder using a solid state memory card that allowed events to be recorded without the need to keep changing a cassette.

It was on one of these that Ellen MacArthur recorded her record-breaking solo non-stop circumnavigation in her trimaran *B&Q* in 2004–2005, allowing her to transmit details of her progress to a waiting world.

Ellen MacArthur pictured aboard *B&Q*, the yacht in which she broke the world record for the fastest solo circumnavigation. She used a camcorder to record many of the ups and downs of her voyage.

99 : CAMCORDER , 2001

# 100 : GoPro

## 2006

The launch of the GoPro miniature waterproof video camera was a major breakthrough in the ability to capture moments of sailing history and action. The GoPro came about through surfer Nick Woodman's desire to capture memorable moments during his surfing exploits at a time when only professional surfers would see their best endeavours captured on camera. He came up with a camera that could be clipped on to a headband or a wristband and ultimately anywhere on a yacht, racing car or any other moving object. The name GoPro was derived from the fact that many surfers nurtured the idea that they would eventually go professional.

Beginning with 10-second digital videos, the technology developed to incorporate a 3-megapixel camera with an SD slot and sound, and eventually a 170-degree wide angle lens that enabled users to create an almost IMAX-like experience along with the mounting system that enabled the camera to be worn or attached almost everywhere. The camera was mounted on everything from cars to helmets to ski poles to boats and eventually to the surfboards that had inspired the product.

Today, the GoPro can be positioned almost anywhere on or under a boat. It was these remote cameras that brought the 2013 America's Cup races in San Francisco Bay between *Oracle Team USA* and *Team New Zealand* 'alive', capturing the spray-filled action like never before and creating a whole new raft of sailing enthusiasts.

Right: A GoPro camera can be fixed to a headband or another point on the wearer's body. Above: A still from footage taken during the Volvo Ocean Race in 2014–2015 using a GoPro chest camera. The crew was able to capture with great immediacy the sheer level of exertion needed to keep one of these yachts sailing to her maximum, without stopping the work.

# Index

## PICTURE CREDITS